An Afternoon Tea Party

CAKES
&
BISCUITS

Photography
Ray Joyce

Illustrations
Barbara Rodanska

LEOPARD

The publisher thanks the following for their assistance in the
photography for this book:

The Glass House, Warringah Mall, Brookvale
Australian Country Life, Sydney Road, Fairlight
Villeroy and Boch, Orchard Road, Brookvale

A NOTE TO COOKS

The recipes in this book use a combination of metric weights
and, for some dry and liquid ingredients, cup measures.
Cooks wishing to use Imperial weights, or who are
unfamiliar with cup measures, should consult the
Conversion Chart before attempting any of the recipes.

COOKERY RATING

easy

a little care needed

for confident cooks

CONTENTS

Chocolate Cakes

for Chocolate Lovers

THERE'S NOTHING QUITE LIKE indulging in an extra special chocolate treat — the rich consistency and ever-moreish flavour of chocolate makes it one of life's great pleasures. Your search for the perfect moist yet light chocolate indulgence is over — this section is chock-full of recipes you won't be able to resist, from the Chocolate Box Cake to the more wholesome Fruity Chocolate Cake.

It might interest you to know that *Theobroma*, the name for the tree which yields chocolate, means 'food of the Gods'.

Family Chocolate Cake, Fruity Chocolate Cake and Glazed Brownies

POINTERS FOR PERFECTION
Scrumptious chocolate cakes can be made with hot chocolate or cocoa powder. The most delicious rich chocolate cakes often call for melted cooking chocolate.

It is important to melt cooking chocolate carefully. Break the chocolate into small pieces, place in a bowl over a saucepan of simmering water — the water should not touch the base of the bowl or boil as this can cause the chocolate to 'seize' or turn into unusable lumps!

Chocolate takes only a few minutes to melt. Once ready, stir briskly, remove from heat then use as directed in recipe.

Chocolate can also be melted in the microwave on Medium (70%) for 2–3 minutes.

While the chocolate is still warm and fluid, add flavourings such as coffee and essences.

You can also enrich the chocolate at this stage with butter, cream or sour cream.

It is at this stage that you can make moulded decorations such as chocolate leaves.

The chocolate needs to be cooled and hardened to make scrolls and cut out shapes.

Glazed Brownies

These cakes are very rich, ideal to serve with coffee after dinner.

PREPARATION TIME: *1¼ hours plus*
standing time
COOKING TIME: *1 hour*
MAKES 36

BASE
60 g cooking chocolate
110 g butter
½ cup plain flour, sifted
1 cup quick-cooking oats
½ cup brown sugar
pinch bicarbonate of soda
FILLING
90 g cooking chocolate
⅔ cup plain flour
¼ teaspoon baking powder
125 g butter, softened
¾ cup sugar
3 eggs
1¼ teaspoons vanilla essence
⅔ cup coarsely chopped walnuts
CHOCOLATE GLAZE
155 g dark chocolate, chopped
3 teaspoons butter
3 tablespoons boiling water
extra walnuts for decoration (optional)

1 Preheat oven to 180°C. Line a 20 cm square baking tin with greaseproof paper and grease paper.

2 To prepare base: melt chocolate and butter in a bowl over simmering water. Mix well. In a small bowl, combine flour, oats, sugar and soda. Add chocolate mixture and mix well. Press evenly into prepared tin and bake for 15 minutes. Set aside and allow to cool slightly.

3 To prepare filling: melt chocolate and cool. Sift together flour and baking powder; set aside. Cream butter and sugar until light and fluffy. Beat in eggs, one at a time. Stir in vanilla essence and cooled chocolate. Fold in flour mixture and walnuts. Spread evenly over partially cooled base. Bake until skewer inserted near centre comes out barely moist, about 35 minutes. Cool.

4 To prepare glaze: blend chocolate, butter and water in a bowl over barely simmering water until smooth. Mix well. Remove from heat and cool to spreading consistency. Spread over cooled filling and leave to cool. Cover and stand for several hours before cutting. Garnish each slice with a walnut, if desired.

When preparing cake tins for chocolate cakes, dust them with sifted cocoa powder in place of flour, as sometimes flour can leave a white dusting over the baked cake.

Chocolate Boxes

These make delicious rich desserts.

PREPARATION TIME: *1 hour
15 minutes plus 30 minutes chilling
time*
COOKING TIME: *1 hour*
MAKES 6 boxes

*155 g butter, chopped
100 g dark chocolate, chopped
1 cup caster sugar
2 tablespoons coffee-flavoured liqueur
2 teaspoons instant coffee powder
1 cup plain flour
¼ cup self-raising flour
2 tablespoons cocoa
2 eggs, lightly beaten
12 x 25 cm lengths ribbon
1 cup cream, whipped
200 g punnet fresh raspberries
CHOCOLATE SQUARES
300 g dark chocolate
30 g butter*

1 Preheat oven to 160°C. For this recipe, use a greased and lined 19 cm square cake tin.

2 Combine butter, chocolate, sugar, liqueur and coffee in heatproof bowl. Stir over saucepan of simmering water until smooth and melted. Remove from heat, stir in sifted flours and cocoa and eggs. Beat well. Pour mixture into tin, bake for 1 hour. Remove from oven; cool. Carefully remove cake from tin and trim edges. Cut into six 4 cm squares.

3 Place 2 lengths of ribbon on each serving plate to form a cross. Place a square of cake in centre of each cross. Spread cream evenly over each cake square.

4 Enclose sides of cake with chocolate squares. Spoon remaining cream onto top of cake squares. Top with raspberries.

5 Place remaining chocolate squares on top of each box to form a lid, as shown.

6 Chill boxes for 30 minutes. Before serving, carefully tie ribbons over top of each box.

7 To prepare Chocolate Squares: melt chocolate and butter in bowl over simmering water. Spread chocolate evenly on foil to form a 25 cm x 30 cm square. Chill until set. Cut into 5 cm squares. You will need 30 squares.

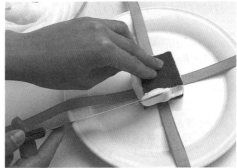

Step 1 Place a square of cake in the centre of each cross. Spread cream evenly over cake, press chocolate squares against sides of cake.

Step 2 Spoon remaining cream onto top of cake squares and top with raspberries.

Step 3 Place remaining chocolate squares carefully on tops of boxes to form lids.

Chocolate is made from the beans of the Cacao tree. The beans are fermented, roasted and ground to a paste. When sugar and cocoa butter are added, the product is called chocolate liquor, which, when hardened, is the chocolate we all enjoy. There are various types of chocolate. Dark, or semi-sweet, is ideal for cooking and decorations. Milk chocolate has the addition of dried milk powder and is delicious as an eating chocolate. White chocolate is essentially a confection of cocoa butter, milk and sugar enjoyed as an eating chocolate. Cooking, or compound, chocolate is an inexpensive form of cooking chocolate best used in baking. For chocolate decorations, use good quality dark chocolate.

When a recipe calls for several dry ingredients to be sifted, do this three times to ensure all ingredients are well dispersed and aerated, so baked goods have a lighter, airier texture.

Family Chocolate Cake

Use after-dinner mints to decorate this cake. Using a small sharp knife, cut mints in half diagonally to form triangles. Place decoratively over cake.

PREPARATION TIME: *50 minutes*
COOKING TIME: *40 minutes*
MAKES 1 CAKE

125 g butter, softened
⅔ cup sugar
⅓ cup icing sugar
1¼ cups self-raising flour
½ cup cocoa
1 teaspoon bicarbonate of soda
2 eggs
1 cup milk
1 teaspoon vanilla essence
pecan halves to decorate
CHOCOLATE ICING
1 cup icing sugar, sifted
1 tablespoon cocoa
1½ tablespoons boiling water
1 teaspoon vanilla essence

1 Preheat oven to 180°C. Grease a 23 cm cake tin, line with greaseproof paper and grease paper.

2 Cream butter with sugar and icing sugar until light and fluffy. Sift flour with cocoa and soda three times into a bowl. Add flour mixture to butter with remaining ingredients and beat together until well blended.

3 Spoon into prepared tin and bake for 40 minutes or until cooked when tested with a skewer. Turn out onto a wire rack to cool.

4 To prepare icing: combine all ingredients in a bowl over simmering water and stir until smooth. Pour over cold cake and spread with a knife dipped in hot water.

Fudge Wedge with Two Sauces

Our Fudge Wedge Cake has a moist dense texture and would be an ideal dessert cake.

PREPARATION TIME: *1 hour*
COOKING TIME: *35 minutes*
MAKES 1 CAKE

125 g butter
125 g dark chocolate, chopped
2 cups brown sugar
1 teaspoon vanilla essence
2 eggs, slightly beaten
1 cup plain flour
¼ teaspoon baking powder
1 cup chopped walnuts, pecans or macadamia nuts
sifted icing sugar for dusting
CHOCOLATE AND VANILLA CUSTARD SAUCES
2 cups cream
4 egg yolks
⅓ cup caster sugar
60 g dark chocolate, melted
2 teaspoons vanilla essence

1 Preheat oven to 180°C. Grease a 20 cm round cake or springform tin, line with greaseproof paper and grease paper.

2 In a small pan, heat butter and chopped chocolate over low heat until just melted and smooth. Add sugar and vanilla. Cook, stirring constantly, until sugar dissolves. Cool slightly then stir in beaten eggs.

3 Sift flour and baking powder three times into a bowl. Thoroughly fold into chocolate mixture, then fold in nuts.

4 Turn mixture into prepared tin, smoothing surface. Bake for 30 minutes until cake pulls from side of tin and a sugary glaze forms on the surface. Cool completely in tin on a wire rack. Just before serving, dust with icing sugar. Cut into wedges and serve with sauces.

5 To prepare sauces: in a pan gently heat cream until boiling. In a bowl beat egg yolks and sugar until blended. Gradually add scalded cream, mixing well.

6 Return mixture to pan. Cook, stirring constantly over low heat, until sauce slightly thickens and coats the spoon (do not boil).

7 Divide sauce equally between two bowls (pouring through a strainer, if lumpy). Stir melted chocolate into one bowl; vanilla into the other bowl. Cover surfaces of sauces directly with plastic wrap. Cool, then chill until needed.

Easy Chocolate Madeira Cake

Our Chocolate Madeira Cake is the perfect partner for a special afternoon tea.

PREPARATION TIME: *50 minutes*
COOKING TIME: *1 hour*
MAKES 1 CAKE

2 cups plain flour, sifted
2 teaspoons baking powder
155 g butter, softened
2 cups sugar
3 teaspoons vanilla essence
2 eggs
⅔ cup sifted cocoa
1¼ cups milk
TOPPING
1 cup icing sugar, sifted
1 teaspoon vanilla essence
2–3 teaspoons water
60 g dark chocolate
1 teaspoon butter

1 Preheat oven to 180°C. Grease and flour a guglhupf or decorative ring tin.

2 Sift together flour and baking powder and set aside. In a medium mixing bowl, beat together butter, sugar and vanilla until fluffy. Add eggs, one at a time, beating well after each addition. Beat in cocoa. Add milk alternately with sifted dry ingredients in three lots, beating well after each addition.

3 Pour into prepared tin and bake for about 1 hour until a skewer inserted in the centre of the cake comes out clean. Cool cake in tin for 2 minutes. Turn out on a wire rack to cool completely.

4 To prepare topping: in a small bowl, stir together sugar, vanilla and enough water to make a smooth glaze. Spoon over top of cooled cake. Cut up chocolate and melt with butter in a bowl over very warm water. Stir until smooth. Drizzle over glaze to make a decorative two-toned pattern.

Stand until set.

If you need to test a cake for doneness and a metal skewer is not available use a fine piece of uncooked spaghetti. Insert spaghetti into centre of cake — it should come out clean if cake is baked.

Fudge Wedge with Two Sauces

Easy Chocolate Madeira Cake

Fruity Chocolate Cake

Replace glacé cherries with other glacé fruits, if desired. A tempting combination could be glacé pears and glacé ginger.

PREPARATION TIME: 40 minutes plus
overnight soaking time
COOKING TIME: 35 minutes
MAKES 2 CAKES

⅓ cup raisins
2 tablespoons brandy
60 g dark chocolate, chopped
125 g butter, softened
1¼ cups caster sugar
2 eggs
1 teaspoon vanilla essence
2 cups self-raising flour
1 teaspoon bicarbonate of soda
1 teaspoon each cinnamon and nutmeg
1 cup milk
⅓ cup chopped glacé cherries
½ cup coarsely chopped walnuts

1 Soak raisins in brandy for several hours or overnight. Preheat oven to 180°C, and grease and flour two 20 cm round sandwich cake tins.

2 Melt chocolate in a bowl over hot water. Allow to cool.

3 Cream butter and sugar until light and fluffy. Beat in eggs one at a time. Add chocolate and vanilla.

4 Sift flour, soda and spices three times into a bowl. Add to creamed mixture alternately with milk. Stir in soaked raisins, cherries and walnuts.

5 Spoon mixture into prepared tins, and bake for 35 minutes or until cooked when tested. Cool in tins for five minutes and finish cooling on wire racks.

White and Dark Truffle Cake

This cake looks wonderful garnished with frosted rose petals. Brush petals lightly with whisked egg white, sprinkle liberally with caster sugar and dry on a wire rack.

PREPARATION TIME: 1½ hours plus
several hours chilling time
COOKING TIME: 30 minutes
MAKES 1 CAKE

2 eggs
¼ cup caster sugar
3 tablespoons cornflour
2 tablespoons cocoa
2 tablespoons cold strong black coffee
1 tablespoon whisky
DARK LAYERS
400 g dark chocolate
2 cups thickened cream
WHITE LAYER
200 g white chocolate
300 ml thickened cream

1 Preheat oven to 190°C. Grease and line the base of a 23 cm springform tin and grease again.

2 In a large bowl over barely simmering water, whisk eggs with sugar for 5–7 minutes until thick and creamy. Remove from heat.

3 Sift cornflour and cocoa three times into a bowl. Fold into egg mixture until no streaks remain. Turn into prepared tin, spreading evenly.

4 Bake for about 7 minutes until risen. Cool 10 minutes in tin. Remove to a cake rack and cool completely. Wash and thoroughly dry the tin; carefully return cooled cake. Combine coffee and whisky and evenly brush or drizzle over cake.

5 To prepare first dark layer: melt half the chocolate in a bowl over simmering water. Cool. Beat half the cream until thick; fold in chocolate until smooth. Spread evenly over cake layer in tin. Bang tin on bench once or twice to remove air bubbles. Place in refrigerator.

6 To prepare white layer: melt white chocolate; remove from heat. Spread a heaped tablespoon onto greaseproof paper and set aside for making curls. Cool remaining chocolate.

7 Beat cream until thick. Fold in cooled white chocolate until smooth. Spread evenly over dark layer in tin. Bang on bench; chill.

8 To prepare second dark layer: prepare as directed in Step 5, using remaining dark layer ingredients. Pour over white layer; bang again, then swirl the surface to decorate. Chill several hours until set.

9 To serve: remove sides of tin. Place cake on a serving plate. Using a sharp knife, shave reserved white chocolate into curls and sprinkle over cake. Cut into very thin slices. Keep refrigerated.

White and Dark Truffle Cake

Butter Cakes

Melt-in-the-mouth

Butter cakes are versatile, light and easy to make, and can be cooked in a variety of pans. They have that wonderfully light texture yet remain moist and keep well, especially the fruity ones. Our Basic Butter Cake has some delicious variations, ideal for morning or afternoon teas. Try a cake with a difference, Banana Cake with Passionfruit Syrup. For something even fruitier, try the Lime Streusel, or the tart and tempting Plum Cake.

Lime Streusel Cake   Banana Cake with Passionfruit Syrup

To test eggs for freshness, place whole eggs in a bowl of cold water. Fresh eggs will sink to the bottom of the bowl and stale eggs will float.

POINTERS FOR PERFECTION
Butter, cooking margarine and some fats can all be used in baking. Butter, however, will give the best result and flavour. To produce excellent results always use unsalted butter. If you are concerned about cholesterol, use a poly-unsaturated margarine, bearing in mind that this will make the cake slightly heavier and denser in texture.

It is important to soften butter when making butter cakes by the creaming method. If possible, leave measured butter out of the refrigerator overnight. If you forget to leave it out or are cooking on the spur of the moment, soften butter by cutting it in about 10 pieces and leaving it in a warm place.

Alternatively, you can place it in the microwave for a few seconds. It is most important that the butter does not melt. Warming the beater and the bowl can also help the softening process.

Basic Butter Cake

The Basic Butter Cake can be cooked in a variety of tins. All tins need to be greased, and for the best results, base lined with paper, then the paper greased (unless using baking paper which doesn't need to be greased). Some fancy tins cannot be lined with paper, as the cake would lose its shape. Grease them with melted butter and sprinkle with plain flour, cornflour or coconut. Generally butter cakes are cooked in a moderate oven at 180°C.

PREPARATION TIME: *40 minutes*
COOKING TIME: *40 minutes*
MAKES 1 CAKE

125 g butter, softened
1 teaspoon vanilla essence
¾ cup caster sugar
2 eggs
1½ cups self-raising flour, sifted
½ cup milk

1 Preheat oven to 180°C and prepare a cake tin of your choice.

2 Cream butter, vanilla and sugar in a small bowl with an electric mixer until light and fluffy. This will take 10 minutes, or 20 minutes by hand using a wooden spoon. Mixture will be pale and light in texture.

3 Beat in eggs, one at a time, beating until combined. Stir in half the flour and half the milk, then stir in remaining flour and milk.

4 Pour mixture into prepared tin and bake for 40 minutes, or use this basic batter as shown in the following recipes.

Banana Cake with Passionfruit Syrup

Canned passionfruit pulp may be substituted for fresh. We used two over-ripe bananas and about seven passionfruit for this recipe. Strain the passionfruit pulp to obtain the passionfruit juice required. Cake can be made up to four days ahead: store in an airtight container.

PREPARATION TIME: *45 minutes*
COOKING TIME: *50 minutes*
MAKES 1 CAKE

CAKE
125 g unsalted butter, softened
1 teaspoon vanilla essence
¾ cup caster sugar
2 eggs
¼ teaspoon bicarbonate of soda
½ cup milk
¾ cup mashed banana
1½ cups self-raising flour, sifted
PASSIONFRUIT SYRUP
¾ cup caster sugar
½ cup water
¼ cup strained passionfruit juice

1 Preheat oven to 180°C. Grease a 20 cm baba tin, sprinkle with flour and shake out excess flour.

2 To prepare cake: cream butter, vanilla and sugar in a small bowl with an electric mixer until light and fluffy. Beat in eggs, one at a time, beating until combined.

3 Dissolve soda in milk. Stir in mashed banana, half the flour and half the milk. Stir in remaining flour and milk.

4 Pour mixture into prepared tin and

bake for 45 minutes. Stand for 3 minutes in tin before turning onto a cake rack.

5 To prepare syrup: combine caster sugar, water and passionfruit juice in a pan. Stir over heat until sugar dissolves. Bring to the boil, then boil for 3 minutes. Remove from heat and pour hot syrup over hot cake.

Lime Streusel Cake

You can substitute lemon rind and lemon slices for lime.

PREPARATION TIME: *50 minutes*
COOKING TIME: *50 minutes*
MAKES 1 CAKE

1 cup desiccated coconut
⅓ cup brown sugar
2 teaspoons grated lime rind
1 quantity Basic Butter Cake batter
(see recipe)
DECORATION (optional)
whipped cream
toasted coconut
lime slices

1 Preheat oven to 180°C and grease a deep 20 cm cake tin.

2 Place coconut in a heavy-based pan and stir over heat until light golden brown. Remove from pan to cool.

3 To make streusel: combine coconut, brown sugar and lime rind in a small bowl. Coat inside of tin with streusel, shake excess back into bowl, and reserve.

4 Spread half the prepared cake batter in tin, then sprinkle evenly with reserved streusel. Using a skewer, swirl streusel through batter, then top with remaining batter.

5 Bake for about 50 minutes, or until firm. Stand cake in tin for five minutes before turning out onto a cake rack to cool.

6 Remove paper when cool. Decorate cake with whipped cream, toasted coconut and lime slices, if desired.

Step 1 Place coconut in a heavy-based pan and stir over heat until light golden brown.

Step 2 Coat inside of tin with streusel, shake excess back into bowl and reserve.

Step 3 Using a skewer, swirl streusel through batter, top with remaining batter.

The origins of the lime are generally unknown. Some believe the fruit was first discovered in China while others suggest Persia or the East Indies. Wherever its origin we can only be grateful for it is perhaps the finest of citrus fruits.

Our early rolling pins were made of sycamore, which does not colour or flavour food. They were used for rolling doughs and pastry, while other rolling pins were ridged to crush oats and salt.

Plum Cake and Walnut Cake

Walnut Cake

You can substitute pecans, almonds and hazelnuts for the walnuts if you wish. Cakes are best frozen unfilled and without icing. Wrap in freezer wrap, bags or foil, excluding as much air as possible. Label and date. Cakes freeze successfully for up to three months.

PREPARATION TIME: *50 minutes*
COOKING TIME: *30 minutes*
MAKES 1 CAKE

CAKE
125 g butter, softened
1 cup caster sugar
3 eggs
1 cup self-raising flour
¼ cup plain flour
¼ cup milk
1 cup finely chopped walnuts
whipped cream
ORANGE ICING
30 g unsalted butter
1¼ cups icing sugar, sifted
1 tablespoon orange juice

1 Preheat oven to 180°C. Grease two 20 cm sandwich cake tins, line with paper and grease paper.

2 To prepare cake: cream butter and sugar in a bowl with an electric mixer until light and fluffy. Beat in eggs, one at a time, beating until combined. Sift together flours and fold in alternately with milk, then fold in walnuts.

3 Pour mixture into prepared tins and bake for about 30 minutes. Stand for 3–4 minutes in tins before turning out onto a cake rack. Remove paper.

4 When cold, join together with whipped cream (add a little grated orange rind, if you wish) and top with icing.

5 To prepare icing: melt butter, stir in icing sugar and orange juice and beat until smooth.

Plum Cake

Some of the plum slices may sink into the cake while cooking, which gives it a more interesting appearance and distributes the plums throughout the cake, making it more delicious.

PREPARATION TIME: *1 hour*
COOKING TIME: *50 minutes*
MAKES 1 CAKE

500 g purple plums, halved and stoned
¾ cup caster sugar or more
125 g unsalted butter, softened
1 teaspoon grated lemon rind
3 eggs, separated
1 cup self-raising flour, sifted

1 Preheat oven to 180°C. Grease a 23 cm springform tin, line base with paper and grease paper.

2 Slice plums thinly and sprinkle with three tablespoons sugar.

3 Cream butter, lemon rind and remaining sugar until light and fluffy.

4 Beat in egg yolks one at a time, beating until combined. Stir in flour. Beat egg whites until stiff then fold into cake mixture.

5 Pour mixture into prepared tin, spreading evenly. Arrange drained plum slices over top and, if they are very tart, sprinkle with 1–2 tablespoons more sugar.

6 Bake for 45–50 minutes. Stand for three minutes in tin before turning out onto a cake rack. Remove paper. Serve for afternoon tea, as a dessert cake with whipped cream or with a light sprinkling of icing sugar.

Sugar-frosted seasonal fruits make impressive garnishes for iced cakes. Dip small clusters of grapes, small plums or apricots in lightly beaten egg white and then in sugar until evenly coated, and leave to dry on greaseproof paper.

Almonds are the dominant nut in world trade. They are used for sweetmeats, cakes, desserts and sauce, while ground almonds are used for thickening and flavouring in soups and meat dishes.

Caramel Cake

If caramel is hard after water is added, return to low heat until dissolved.

PREPARATION TIME: *1½ hours*
COOKING TIME: *35 minutes*
MAKES 1 CAKE

CARAMEL SYRUP
1 cup sugar
¾ cup boiling water
CAKE
185 g butter, softened
½ cup brown sugar
3 eggs, separated
1 teaspoon vanilla essence
3 cups self-raising flour, sifted
¾ cup of milk
pecan halves and chopped pecans to decorate
FROSTING
125 g unsalted butter, softened
500 g icing sugar, sifted
1½ teaspoons vanilla essence

1 Preheat oven to 180°C. Grease two 23 cm sandwich tins, line with paper and grease paper.

2 Make the syrup first: heat sugar in a heavy pan over very low heat, stirring until melted and a rich caramel colour. Remove from heat and cool to room temperature. Add boiling water, and heat gently over medium heat until caramelised sugar melts in the water. Remove from heat and cool before using.

3 To prepare cake: cream butter and sugar until light and fluffy. Beat in egg yolks and vanilla, beating until combined. Gradually beat in ½ cup syrup.

4 Stir in flour alternately with milk. Beat egg whites until stiff, and fold lightly through mixture.

5 Pour mixture into prepared tins and bake for 35 minutes until cooked. Turn onto a cake rack. Remove paper.

6 To make frosting: cream butter and icing sugar until light and fluffy. Gradually beat in ¼ cup caramel syrup and then vanilla, beating well.

7 When cakes are quite cold, join together with half the frosting, and ice all over with remaining frosting. Decorate with pecan halves and chopped pecans.

Sand Cake

This very rich, plain cake is known in Russia and the Baltic as 'Livia Kook'. Its unusual sand-like texture is due to the potato flour and finely chopped almonds. This cake is also one of the nicest butter cakes in many a cook's repertoire.

PREPARATION TIME: *50 minutes*
COOKING TIME: *1½ hours*
MAKES 1 CAKE

250 g unsalted butter, softened
¾ cup caster sugar
2 teaspoons brandy
½ teaspoon vanilla essence
3 eggs
1 cup plain flour
1 cup potato flour
1½ teaspoons baking powder
¼ cup finely chopped blanched almonds
sifted icing sugar (optional)

1 Preheat oven to 180°C. Grease a deep-sided 20 cm cake tin, line with paper and grease paper.

2 Cream butter, sugar, brandy and vanilla until light and fluffy. Beat in eggs, one at a time, beating well until combined.

3 Sift together three times plain and potato flours and baking powder. Add to creamed mixture, mixing until smooth. Stir in almonds.

4 Pour mixture into prepared tin, spreading evenly. Bake for 1–1½ hours until golden brown and edges barely pull from sides of tin. Cool in tin five minutes before turning out onto cake rack. Remove paper.

5 Dust lightly with icing sugar, if desired. Slice and serve with butter.

Sand Cake and Caramel Cake

A GUIDE TO PERFECT CAKES

To ACHIEVE SUCCESS each time with baking you need to look to your basic ingredients. The best cakes start with the best ingredients, each of which plays a specific part.

Flour gives body to the cake, butter and sugar flavour and tenderise it, eggs contribute to the framework of the cake, and the liquid (which is usually milk, sour cream or a combination of both) develops the starch and gluten in the flour.

Getting It Right

Follow these guidelines to ensure success each time.
- Use the freshest ingredients;
- Weigh or measure ingredients accurately. Don't ever try to judge quantities by eye, but use standard measuring cups and spoons;
- Follow the steps of the recipe carefully;
- Choose the correct size tin and prepare the cake tin as directed;
- Check oven temperature and avoid opening oven door until at least two-thirds of the way through cooking.

Baking Times

Baking times will vary slightly according to your oven, and types of baking ware. Use the times given as a guide only (you should start checking a cake about two-thirds of the way through cooking).

When is a Cake Ready?

A cooked cake should have an even colour, be firm when touched in the centre and should shrink away from the sides of the tin. The final test is to insert a fine skewer into the centre of the cake — if it comes out clean, the cake is cooked.

Cooling the Cake

Unless the recipe states otherwise, remove the cooked cake to a wire cake rack and cool on the rack in the tin for a short while (4–5 minutes for plain cakes, 10 minutes for fruit cakes and other rich cakes) before carefully turning out. Leave on the rack until completely cold.

Causes of Problems

A Close Texture
Too much liquid;
Insufficient creaming of butter and sugar;
Mixture curdled when eggs were added resulting in loss of air.

Cakes Sunk in the Middle
Too much sugar;
Mixture too wet, too little flour;
Oven too cool;
Oven too hot — this makes the cake appear to be cooked on the outside before cooking in the centre;
Insufficient baking time.

Surface Cracking on Cakes
Too much flour;
Too little liquid;
Too high an oven temperature;
Cake overbaked.

A Coarse Texture
Under or over mixing of cake;
Too much butter;
Too much sugar.

HOW TO PREPARE CAKE TINS

CAKE TINS COME in all shapes and sizes, including interesting fluted tins that make even a plain cake look special. Spring form tins are invaluable for the easy release of delicate cakes. Some tins, although they seem to be different sizes, actually hold the same volume. To substitute one tin for another, measure the amount of batter and then pour the same amount of water into the tin you want to use. If the water doesn't come more than two thirds of the way up the tin you can use it. Most cake tins are filled at least half full, but not more than two thirds, unless the recipe requires it.

GREASING A CAKE TIN. Melt a little butter and, using a pastry brush, coat the inside of the cake tin with butter. This will give the cake an even-textured consistent appearance when it is turned out.

If the recipe says, 'grease and dust with flour', grease the tin first, then sprinkle a little flour over the base and sides. Rotate the tin so the flour clings evenly to the greased surface, then turn upside down and tap lightly on the bench to shake out excess flour.

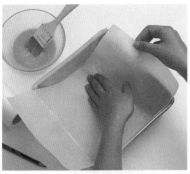

1. *To Line a Square Cake Tin*
Cut a length of grease-proof paper large enough to cover base and two sides. Repeat with second sheet of paper at right angles.

2. *To Line a Round Tin*
Cut piece of grease-proof paper long enough to go round side of tin. Fold over 3 cm along edge of paper and make diagonal cuts up to fold.

3. *Gently press strip into greased cake tin along fold.*

4. *Cut paper into round to fit base of tin. Place circle in base of tin.*

Fruit and Vegetable Cakes

Wholesome and Nutritious

WHOLESOME AND NUTRITIOUS fruit and vegetable cakes are always in demand — they look great and will keep you looking good too. We have included a rich selection of moist, healthy and hearty cakes for all tastes and skills. Try our classic Apple Cake, Spicy Carrot Cake, or — for a more colourful splash — the Orange Pumpkin cake.

Cakes based on a fruit or vegetable usually have a better flavour and texture a day or two after cooking. If the weather is humid, make sure you refrigerate your cake in an airtight container — it will last much longer.

Pineapple Slices and Orange Pumpkin Cake

To use honey instead of sugar in a recipe, for each cup of sugar, substitute ¾ cup of honey and reduce the liquid in the recipe by ¼ cup. Reduce baking temperature by 15°C. Crystallisation: if kept cold, pure liquid honey will form crystals. Simply immerse the container in warm water until the crystals melt; return creamed honey to its liquid form in the same way.

POINTERS FOR PERFECTION

When using apples in fruit and vegetable cakes use the Granny Smith variety for a moist result.

Always use over ripe bananas when called for and mash with a fork to make up required amount.

If using a mashed vegetable in a recipe, boil, steam or microwave, drain and mash without using butter or milk.

Do not peel zucchini or carrot and grate on a medium sized grater for vegetable cakes.

Make sure fruit and vegetables are at room temperature before mixing with other ingredients.

Fruit and vegetable cakes lend themselves to cream cheese frostings and citrus flavoured syrups making them sinfully sweet.

Apple Cake

Our moist Apple Cake is best eaten on the day of baking. The honey gives it a rich flavour.

PREPARATION TIME: *50 minutes*
COOKING TIME: *55 minutes*
MAKES 1 CAKE

1 ¾ cups wholemeal self-raising flour
1 teaspoon cinnamon
¼ teaspoon nutmeg
2 green apples, peeled, cored and diced
90 g butter, softened
¾ cup brown sugar
2 eggs
½ cup plain yoghurt
1 extra apple, peeled, cored and cut in 8 wedges
2 teaspoons cinnamon
2 teaspoons caster sugar
1 tablespoon honey, warmed

1 Preheat oven to 180°C and grease a 23 cm springform cake tin.

2 Sift flour and spices three times into a bowl with roughage left in sifter. Stir in diced apples. Beat butter and brown sugar until light and creamy. Beat in eggs one at a time. Add flour mixture alternately with yoghurt. Stir until combined.

3 Spoon mixture into prepared tin. Dust apple wedges with combined cinnamon and sugar and push into batter, spoke fashion. Bake for 50–55 minutes. Cool slightly and remove from tin. Brush with warm honey while still hot.

Step 1 Beat in eggs one at a time, beating well after each addition.

Step 2 Dust apple wedges with cinnamon and sugar, carefully push into batter.

Step 3 Arrange apples in a spoke fashion over batter.

Pineapple Slices

Instead of covering with frosting, slice may be brushed with warmed honey or dusted with icing sugar if you prefer.

PREPARATION TIME: *40 minutes*
COOKING TIME: *35 minutes*
MAKES ABOUT 20 SLICES

4 carrots, shredded
¾ cup vegetable oil
¾ cup honey
3 eggs, beaten
¼ cup drained, canned crushed pineapple
2 cups self-raising wholemeal flour
125 g ground hazelnuts
2 teaspoons mixed spice
TOPPING
250 g cream cheese, softened
¼ cup drained, canned crushed pineapple
1 tablespoon honey

1 Preheat oven to 180°C. Grease a 30 x 25 cm baking tin and line with baking paper.

2 In a large bowl, combine carrots, oil, honey, eggs and pineapple. Mix well. Sift together flour, hazelnuts and spice three times. Add roughage left in sifter. Stir into carrot mixture with a wooden spoon until blended.

3 Turn batter into prepared tin, spreading evenly. Bake 30–35 minutes until a skewer inserted in the centre comes out clean. Briefly cool in tin, turn out onto a wire rack and cool completely.

4 To prepare topping: in a bowl use an electric mixer to beat cream cheese, pineapple and honey. Spread over top of cake. Chill until needed. Cut into slices to serve.

Orange Pumpkin Cake

If weather is humid store Pumpkin Cake in an airtight container in refrigerator. Serve at room temperature.

PREPARATION TIME: *40 minutes*
COOKING TIME: *1 hour*
MAKES 1 CAKE

125 g butter
2 teaspoons grated orange rind
¾ cup sugar

1 cup mashed pumpkin
1 cup sultanas
2 cups self-raising flour, sifted
½ cup milk
ORANGE ICING
1 cup icing sugar, sifted
2 teaspoons butter
1 tablespoon orange juice

1 Preheat oven to 180°C. Grease a 20 cm deep-sided cake tin, line with greaseproof paper and grease paper.

2 Beat together butter, orange rind, sugar and pumpkin. Mix in sultanas then fold in sifted flour alternately with milk.

3 Turn into prepared tin and bake for about one hour or until cooked when tested. Turn out onto a cake rack to cool completely and remove paper.

4 To prepare icing: heat all ingredients in a small pan, stirring over gentle heat until butter melts and ingredients combine. Spread evenly over cake and serve.

Pineapples do not ripen after harvesting, but change in colouring and soften owing to respiration and acid loss. Choose a pineapple that is plump and heavy in relation to its size. A fragrant smell is a good indication. A musty, beery smell means it is overripe.

Apple Cake

Mixed spice is also known as pudding spice. It is a blend of allspice, cinnamon, nutmeg, mace and cloves, and may also contain pepper or coriander.

Spicy Carrot Cake

Serve our Spicy Carrot Cake with warmed custard as a winter dessert.

PREPARATION TIME: *25 minutes*
COOKING TIME: *45 minutes*
MAKES 1 CAKE

1 cup plain flour
1 teaspoon baking powder
1 teaspoon bicarbonate of soda
1 teaspoon mixed spice
1 teaspoon nutmeg
⅔ cup sunflower or safflower oil
⅔ cup sugar
2 eggs, beaten
½ cup chopped nuts
1 large carrot, grated
CITRUS GLAZE
½ cup icing sugar, sifted
1 teaspoon grated lemon rind
1 tablespoon lemon juice

1 Preheat oven to 180°C, grease and flour a 20 cm square cake tin.

2 Sift flour, baking powder, bicarbonate and spices three times into a bowl. Combine oil, sugar and beaten eggs. Stir into flour mixture.

3 Add nuts and grated carrot and blend well. Spoon into prepared tin and bake for 45 minutes, or until cooked when tested. Turn out and brush top and sides with glaze while hot.

4 To prepare glaze: combine icing sugar, lemon rind and lemon juice. Use at once.

Special Banana Cake

This quick and easy banana cake has excellent keeping qualities. Top with a cream cheese frosting and it is sure to be a family favourite.

PREPARATION TIME: *30 minutes*
COOKING TIME: *45 minutes*
MAKES 1 CAKE

1 cup wholemeal plain flour
1 cup white plain flour
1 teaspoon bicarbonate of soda
1 teaspoon cinnamon
¾ cup brown sugar
½ cup chopped nuts
2 eggs

⅔ cup vegetable oil
½ cup mashed ripe banana
¾ cup each shredded zucchini and carrot

1 Preheat oven to 180°C and grease a 22 cm guglhupf tin.

2 Sift flours, soda and cinnamon three times into a bowl. Stir in sugar and nuts.

3 Beat eggs, oil and banana until smooth. Pour over flour mixture. Add vegetables. Beat until blended.

4 Spoon into prepared tin and bake for 45 minutes until brown and firm. Cool before serving.

Pumpkin Date Nut Loaf

For best results drain pumpkin well and mash without butter or milk.

PREPARATION TIME: *30 minutes*
COOKING TIME: *50 minutes*
MAKES 1 LOAF

30 g melted butter
2 tablespoons finely crushed wheatmeal biscuit crumbs
1¼ cups plain flour
1 teaspoon baking powder
1 teaspoon bicarbonate of soda
1 teaspoon cinnamon
1 teaspoon ground cloves
½ teaspoon ground ginger
1 cup mashed cooked pumpkin
2 eggs
½ cup brown sugar
½ cup caster sugar
½ cup vegetable oil
½ cup chopped pitted dates
½ cup chopped pecans or walnuts
sifted icing sugar to decorate

1 Grease a loaf tin liberally with melted butter. Coat tin with biscuit crumbs and set aside.

2 Sift together flour, baking powder, soda and spices three times into a bowl. In a large bowl, beat together pumpkin, eggs, sugars and oil until blended.

3 Stir in flour mixture until combined. Fold in dates and nuts. Turn into prepared tin. Bake for 45–50 minutes.

4 Stand 10 minutes. Turn out and cool completely on a wire rack.

Pumpkin Date Nut Loaf , Spicy Carrot Cake and Special Banana Cake

Lovely Muffins

Lovely Muffins

To freeze muffins, cool completely. Wrap airtight in plastic or foil, then place in freezer bags. Label, date and freeze up to three months. To thaw, let stand at room temperature until free of frost. Heat foil-wrapped muffins at 160°C for 10–12 minutes.

PREPARATION TIME: *15 minutes*
COOKING TIME: *25 minutes*
MAKES 12

1¾ cups self-raising flour
2–3 tablespoons caster sugar
1 teaspoon baking powder

1 egg, slightly beaten
¾ cup milk
⅓ cup butter, melted

1 Preheat oven to 200°C. Brush oil into bottoms only of twelve 6 cm muffin tin cups. (Unoiled sides allow batter to climb and form rounded tops while baking.)

2 Sift flour, sugar and baking powder three times in a bowl. In a small bowl, combine egg, milk and melted butter. Add liquids all at once to flour mixture.

3 With a fork, stir gently until all dry ingredients are just moistened. Batter should look quite lumpy. (Overmixing results in rubbery muffins with peaked tops and long holes or tunnels inside.)

4 Scoop batter into each muffin cup, filling two-thirds full. Bake 20–25 minutes until golden brown. Loosen muffins with a spatula and remove at once to a wire rack. Serve warm.

Variations

1 Almond Chip Muffins: prepare as directed above, but add 2 teaspoons grated lemon peel, ½ teaspoon vanilla essence, and ¾ cup chopped unblanched almonds to liquids before mixing with flour mixture.

2 Citrus Sugar Muffins: prepare as directed above, but add 3 teaspoons each grated orange and lemon (or lime) peel to liquids before mixing with flour mixture. Brush hot baked muffins with extra melted butter. Sprinkle with caster sugar and garnish with thin strips of citrus peel.

3 Blueberry Bran Muffins: prepare as directed above, but stir ¼ cup unprocessed bran into sifted dry ingredients. Add ½ teaspoon vanilla essence to liquids before mixing with flour mixture. Fold a generous cupful of fresh (or unsweetened frozen, slightly thawed) blueberries or blackcurrants into batter before baking.

4 Apple-sauce Muffins: prepare as directed above, but increase eggs to 2 and substitute 1 cup apple sauce for the milk. Fold ½ cup chopped walnuts or pecans into batter before baking.

5 Apricot and Ginger Muffins: prepare as directed above, but add 1½ teaspoons ground ginger to dry ingredients before sifting. Add ¾ cup finely chopped dried apricots and 1½ teaspoons grated lemon peel to liquids before mixing with flour mixture.

Carrot Nut Ring

Any combination of nuts may be used for this cake. Take care when turning cake out.

PREPARATION TIME: *50 minutes*
COOKING TIME: *50 minutes*
MAKES 1 CAKE

90 g butter
½ cup caster sugar
2 eggs
1½ cups self-raising flour, sifted
¼ cup milk
½ cup grated carrot
¼ cup chopped walnuts
¼ cup chopped unblanched almonds
¼ cup chopped glacé cherries
TOPPING
2 tablespoons chopped walnuts
2 tablespoons chopped unblanched almonds
2 tablespoons chopped glacé cherries
2 tablespoons sugar

1 Preheat oven to 180°C and grease a 20 cm ring tin.

2 Beat together butter and sugar until creamy. Add eggs, one at a time, beating well after each addition. Stir in flour alternately with milk.

3 Add carrot, walnuts, almonds and cherries, beating with a wooden spoon until thoroughly mixed. Spread evenly in prepared tin.

4 To prepare topping: combine all ingredients in a bowl. Sprinkle topping over cake batter and bake for 40–50 minutes. Leave in tin for 5 minutes then carefully turn out.

Note: this cake freezes well.

Carrot Nut Ring

Sugar & Spice

and All Things Nice . . .

SPICE CAKES HAVE ALWAYS BEEN family favourites. The spices most used are nutmeg, cinnamon, cloves, cardamom, ginger and, of course, mixed spice (not to be confused with allspice).

Buy good quality spices. Store in a dark cupboard and keep for only six months as they become stale and won't give that fresh spicy flavour to your cakes and biscuits.

You can also buy whole nutmegs and grate a little each time you require this wonderful spice.

Somerset Seed Cake (page 37)

POINTERS FOR PERFECTION

Most spices are sold dried, either whole or ground. For the strongest flavour buy whole spices and grind when you need them.

Use a pestle and mortar, hand held grater, or coffee grinder.

Store spices in an airtight container in a cool, dark place.

Sugar and spice cakes are tea time treats and are generally best enjoyed on the day of baking. Serve warm with a dusting of icing sugar and cream. Or slice and serve with lashings of butter.

Essences are also concentrated flavourings. True essences are made by extracting the natural flavours from the food itself, a good example being vanilla from the vanilla bean. True essences have strong flavours and only a small amount is needed in each recipe.

Spices are prime sources of flavour for cakes, biscuits and slices. Nutmeg, cinnamon, cloves and ginger feature in many classic recipes. The spices of the East are now also popular; cardamom, cumin and anise may be substituted for each other. Pepper can also be found in baking, counterbalancing sweet spices.

Cinnamon Honey Cake

Our Cinnamon Honey Cake is very easy to make and bake, perfect to team with afternoon tea.

PREPARATION TIME: *30 minutes*
COOKING TIME: *30 minutes*
MAKES 1 CAKE

¼ cup brown sugar
3 tablespoons honey
1 cup self-raising flour, sifted
1 teaspoon cinnamon
1 egg
60 g butter, softened
⅓ cup milk
LEMON ICING
2 cups icing sugar, sifted
30 g butter, softened
grated rind of 1 lemon
1 tablespoon lemon juice

1 Preheat oven to 180°C and grease a 20 cm sandwich cake tin.

2 Place all ingredients in a bowl and beat well for 4–5 minutes until smooth. Pour into prepared tin and bake for 30 minutes until cooked.

3 Ice when cool with lemon icing and sprinkle with lemon rind.

4 To prepare icing: combine all ingredients in a bowl and beat until light and fluffy. If mixture is too thick, thin with a little hot water.

Plantation Prune Cake

You can store this cake in the freezer, without icing and wrapped in freezer wrap, for up to two months.

PREPARATION TIME: *40 minutes*
COOKING TIME: *1 hour*
MAKES 1 CAKE

2½ cups self-raising flour
1 teaspoon allspice
1 teaspoon cinnamon
1 teaspoon nutmeg
1 cup finely chopped walnuts
3 eggs
1 cup sugar
1 cup vegetable oil
½ cup buttermilk
1 cup chopped soft prunes
VANILLA GLAZE
1 cup sugar
½ cup buttermilk
1 tablespoon light corn syrup (or liquid glucose)
125 g butter
1 teaspoon vanilla essence

1 Preheat oven to 180°C. Grease a 25 cm fluted ring cake tin and flour, shaking out any excess.

2 Sift flour, allspice, cinnamon and nutmeg into a bowl. Stir in walnuts.

3 Beat eggs well in the large bowl of an electric mixer at high speed. Slowly beat in sugar until mixture is fluffy. Fold through vegetable oil, buttermilk and prunes. Fold in flour mixture, a third at a time, until well blended. Pour into prepared tin.

4 Bake for one hour or until top springs back when lightly pressed with fingertip. Cool 10 minutes in tin on a wire rack. Loosen cake around the edges with a knife, turn out onto rack and cool.

5 To prepare glaze: combine all ingredients except vanilla in a pan. Heat slowly, stirring constantly until boiling. Cook, stirring constantly, for two minutes. Remove from heat and stir in vanilla.

6 While hot, drizzle glaze slowly over cake, spooning any that drips onto plate back over cake. Allow icing to set before slicing.

Plantation Prune Cake and Cinnamon Honey Cake

Moist Finnish Cake

Moist Finnish Cake

Avoid using light sour cream, as the cake would have a different texture, due to a lower fat content. This batter is excellent as a substitute for pastry in fruit-topped flans. Pour into a prepared flan tin, bake as directed and top with custard and fruit.

Cardamom is a very aromatic spice from Asia — the world's most expensive spice after saffron. Cardamom is available as whole pods or as a ground spice and is used to flavour both sweet and savoury dishes.

PREPARATION TIME: *25 minutes*
COOKING TIME: *40 minutes*
MAKES 1 CAKE

1 egg
1 cup sour cream
¾ cup caster sugar
1 teaspoon almond essence

1½ cups plain flour
½ teaspoon bicarbonate of soda
½ teaspoon ground cardamom
icing sugar for dusting

1 Preheat oven to 180°C. Grease a 20 cm round cake tin, line with greaseproof paper and grease paper.

2 Place egg, sour cream, sugar and almond essence in the bowl of an electric mixer. Beat until pale and evenly mixed.

3 Sift dry ingredients three times and fold into mixture.

4 Pour mixture into prepared tin and bake for about 40 minutes or until cooked. Cool 10 minutes before removing from tin. Sprinkle top with sifted icing sugar or decorate with cream and fruit.

Somerset Seed Cake

Seed cakes are always a tempting tea time cake. Serve ours with a dusting of icing sugar.

PREPARATION TIME: *35 minutes*
COOKING TIME: *1 hour*
MAKES 1 CAKE

185 g butter
¾ cup caster sugar
2 teaspoons caraway seeds
3 eggs, separated
1 tablespoon ground almonds
2 cups self-raising flour
2 tablespoons milk
extra caraway seeds

1 Preheat oven to 180°C. Grease a 15 cm x 25 cm loaf tin, line with grease-proof paper and grease paper.

2 Cream butter and sugar until light and fluffy. Stir in seeds. Beat egg whites until fairly stiff, add yolks and whisk lightly. Fold into creamed mixture with almonds.

3 Sift flour and fold in alternately with the milk. Pour mixture into prepared tin. Top with a light sprinkling of caraway seeds.

4 Bake for about one hour, or until done when tested. Leave in tin for 10 minutes, then turn out to cool on a wire cake rack. Remove paper and serve.

Spiced Banana Cake

Choose bananas that are really over-ripe (not rotten) to get the best flavour. Add a handful of chopped walnuts for a variation in flavour and texture.

PREPARATION TIME: *40 minutes*
COOKING TIME: *45 minutes*
MAKES 1 CAKE

2 cups brown sugar
1 cup self-raising flour
1 cup plain flour
2 teaspoons mixed spice
125 g butter, cut in pieces
½ teaspoon bicarbonate of soda
½ cup buttermilk
½ cup well-mashed bananas
1 egg, beaten

1 Preheat oven to 180°C and grease a 23 cm square sandwich cake tin.

2 Sift sugar, flours and spice three times into a mixing bowl. Rub in butter pieces until mixture resembles crumbs. Press half the mixture into prepared tin.

3 Dissolve soda in buttermilk. Stir in mashed bananas and beaten egg. Beat this mixture into remaining half of the crumb mixture and pour into prepared tin.

4 Bake for 40–45 minutes. Leave for 5–10 minutes in tin and then carefully turn out on a wire cake rack to cool.

Seed cakes are a variation of the classic Madeira Cake, rich with eggs and butter and traditionally served with a glass of Madeira wine.

Spiced Banana Cake

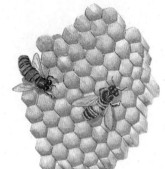

Honey Spice Ring

Substitute two teaspoons of ground ginger in place of cinnamon or cardamom for a honey ginger cake.

PREPARATION TIME: *25 minutes*
COOKING TIME: *1 hour*
MAKES 1 CAKE

2 cups plain flour
¼ teaspoon bicarbonate of soda
1 teaspoon cinnamon
1 teaspoon ground cardamom
¼ teaspoon ground cloves
3 eggs
¾ cup brown sugar
¾ cup honey
¼ cup vegetable oil

Honey Spice Ring

¼ cup marmalade

1 Preheat oven to 180°C and grease a 20 cm ring cake tin.

2 Sift flour, soda and spices three times into a mixing bowl.

3 Add all remaining ingredients and beat at medium speed with an electric mixer for five minutes, scraping down sides of bowl occasionally.

4 Turn batter into prepared tin and bake for 20 minutes. Reduce oven temperature to 160°C. Continue baking for 35–40 minutes until cooked when tested.

5 Turn out onto a wire rack and stand for 15 minutes before removing tin. Cool completely. Wrap in waxed paper and store overnight before cutting the cake. Serve plain or with a thin lemon icing.

Wholemeal and Honey Scones

Serve Wholemeal and Honey Scones straight from the oven with lashings of butter.

PREPARATION TIME: *20 minutes*
COOKING TIME: *15 minutes*
MAKES 8

2 cups wholemeal self-raising flour
1 cup self-raising flour
1 teaspoon cinnamon
¼ teaspoon nutmeg
¾ cup milk
2 tablespoons honey
45 g butter, melted
milk for glazing
sunflower seed kernels, sesame seeds
or oats

1 Preheat oven to 225°C and grease a baking tray.

2 Sift flours and spices into a bowl. Add rough fibre of wholemeal flour to bowl. Combine milk, honey and melted butter. Stir into dry ingredients and mix to a soft dough with a dinner knife.

3 Turn out on a lightly floured surface and knead gently. Shape dough into a 20 cm round and place on prepared tray.

4 With a floured knife, cut completely through to bottom to make eight wedges. Separate wedges slightly. Brush top with a little milk to glaze. Sprinkle with sunflower kernels, sesame seeds or oats, and bake for 15 minutes or until pale golden.

5 Remove from oven and wrap in a clean tea-towel for 10 minutes before serving warm.

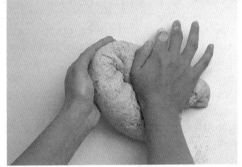

Step 1 Turn dough onto a lightly floured surface, knead gently.

Step 4 Shape dough into a 20 cm round. Cut completely through to make eight wedges.

Traditionally a scone is triangular in shape, made by shaping dough into a round and cutting into triangular sections from the centre. Nowadays they are cut into small rounds and served with fruity jam and cream, a combination known throughout the world as a Devonshire tea.

Wholemeal and Honey Scones

ICINGS TO BRING OUT THE BEST

BUTTERCREAMS MAKE excellent fillings and coverings for cakes. Cakes covered with buttercream remain moist and fresh for longer than cakes left uniced.

Buttercreams can range from a mixture of icing sugar, butter and flavourings to rich elaborate combinations of butter, egg yolks and sugar syrups resulting in a smooth velvety filling.

The secret of making good buttercreams is to use unsalted butter and to beat thoroughly until you make a light creamy mixture.

Glacé icing is a shiny glossy icing which gives a simple finish to cakes and biscuits. Mix icing sugar with a little liquid, such as water, fruit juice or flavourings, and warm slightly until icing becomes smooth and runny. Pour warm icing over the cake, guiding it to give a smooth, even covering. It is important to allow icing to set undisturbed, to prevent the icing from cracking. If you wish to use glacé icing for piping, avoid warming it and keep it as a firm paste.

Vienna Buttercream

PREPARATION TIME: *15 minutes*
COOKING TIME: *Nil*
MAKES Enough for 1 cake

100 g unsalted butter, softened
250 g icing sugar, sifted
2 tablespoons hot water
1 teaspoon vanilla essence

1 Cream butter in a bowl. Gradually beat in sifted icing sugar and continue beating until mixture is light and fluffy.

2 Add hot water and vanilla and beat well. Use as a frosting or to fill cakes and biscuits.

Variations
Chocolate: beat in 60 g melted dark chocolate with the hot water and omit the vanilla.
Coffee: dissolve 1 tablespoon instant coffee powder in the hot water.
Choc-mint: beat in 60 g melted dark chocolate with the hot water. Substitute peppermint essence for the vanilla, and for a special touch, add a 60 g chocolate mint crisp bar that has been crushed.

Vanilla Buttercream

PREPARATION TIME: *10 minutes*
COOKING TIME: *Nil*
MAKES Enough to fill and cover a 22 cm cake

250 g unsalted butter, softened
250 g icing sugar, sifted
2 egg yolks, beaten
2 teaspoons boiling water
vanilla essence

1 Beat together butter and 2 tablespoons of icing sugar until light, fluffy and pale.

2 Add remaining icing sugar gradually, beating well between additions. Beat in egg yolks and boiling water and whisk until blended and smooth.

3 Flavour with vanilla to taste.

Warmed Glacé Icing

PREPARATION TIME: *10 minutes*
COOKING TIME: *2 minutes*
MAKES Enough for 1 cake

360 g pure icing sugar, sifted
1 tablespoon apple juice
4 tablespoons water
1 teaspoon white rum (optional)
food colouring

1 Place icing sugar in a heatproof bowl. Mix liquids together and add gradually to icing sugar to form a smooth spreadable consistency.

2 Place bowl over a dish of boiling water or heat over a pan of simmering water. When icing becomes soft and runny with a shiny appearance, remove from heat.

3 To coat a cake: place cake on a cake rack cooler with the flat side placed underneath. Pour warm icing over cake, using a palette knife or spatula to guide it. Allow the excess to drip off. After icing starts to set, do not touch it until set.

DECORATED CAKES

SIMPLE ICINGS AND BUTTERCREAMS transform plain cakes into special treats. Beautiful icing and decoration take time and patience but the results are well worth it. Glacé icing and buttercream are delicious toppings for buttercakes, and you can vary their flavours by the simple addition of essences, liqueurs, chocolate or citrus. After icing your cake, add some simple decorations to make it even more tempting. Try sugar frosted or chocolate dipped fresh seasonal fruits; use contrasting coloured icings; press finely chopped nuts, toasted coconut or praline onto the sides of the cake; or decorate with very thin slices of poached orange glazed with apricot jam. These suggestions are but a few to show how, with practice and patience, you can turn the most ordinary cake into a masterpiece.

Feathered Icing

If first layer of icing has set before piping over contrasting icing, run a warmed wet palette knife over to resoften first layer.

PREPARATION TIME: *15 minutes*
COOKING TIME: *2 minutes*
MAKES Any quantity

glacé icing (see recipe)

1 Make up enough glacé icing to cover the top of the cake to be iced.

2 Remove approximately 1 tablespoon of prepared icing and tint a contrasting colour to the glacé icing. Place in a piping bag with a size O tube fitted, or alternatively, place in a greaseproof paper icing bag which has had only the tip cut off.

3 Ice cake with the larger portion of icing and while still wet, pipe lines of contrasting icing over the damp icing at 2–3 cm intervals. Turn the cake around so the lines are running horizontally across the cake.

4 Draw a fine skewer across the cake at 2–3 cm intervals. Turn cake around and draw skewer across cake in the opposite direction to form a feather pattern.

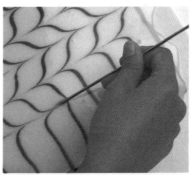

Draw a skewer across the icing at 2–3 cm intervals. Turn the cake around and repeat the process in the opposite direction.

Flaked Almond Decoration

PREPARATION TIME: *15 minutes*
COOKING TIME: *5 minutes*
MAKES enough for 1 x 20 cm cake

180 g flaked almonds

1 Place almonds evenly over baking tray and bake in a moderate oven (180°C) for about 5 minutes or until light golden brown.

2 Take a generous tablespoon of the toasted almonds in the palm of your hand and press them lightly and evenly onto the buttercream on the side of cake.

Press almonds gently to the side of the cake.

Sponge Cakes

Light and Luscious

THE LIGHT AND AIRY SPONGE CAKE is an international favourite — in France, they have Génoise sponge, in Italy Pane di Spagence; the English sponge is sandwiched with jam in the centre, while in Australia, sponges are crowned with lashings of fresh whipped cream and fruits.

The delicate mixture of a sponge depends on the amount of air you beat into the mixture. Show how 'light-handed' you are with a luscious sponge which positively floats.

Strawberry Cake

Pointers for Perfection

Sponge cakes do not keep well, so make them the day you intend to serve them. Although they have the reputation of being difficult to make, you should have no difficulties if you use the following techniques.

Use a clean, dry bowl, fresh eggs and caster sugar.

Sift dry ingredients together three times to incorporate air.

When whisking eggs with sugar, use an electric mixer for at least 10 minutes, so mixture is thick enough to form a 'ribbon' on the surface when lifting mixer. If separating whites, make sure there are not traces of yolk or the white will not form 'peaks'.

Fold dry ingredients into mixture with a metal spoon, gently lifting mixture from bottom of the bowl — do not overmix.

Grease cake tins lightly and dust with flour, preferably cornflour as this gives the cake a fine crust.

Test sponge by lightly touching its top — if it springs back it is ready (avoid testing with a skewer as this can make the sponge drop in the middle).

Handle a hot cooked sponge as little as possible — use a knife to loosen cake in tin and turn out onto a tea-towel placed over a cake rack.

Until the late seventeenth century eggs and egg whites were whisked in a bowl with a bunch of birch or twigs bound to make a brush. Iron wire balloon-shaped whisks were marketed in the mid-eighteenth century. Copper bowls were also introduced to the kitchen. Housewives soon discovered the benefits of the balloon whisk and copper bowl in baking feather light cakes.

Icings and Fillings

GLACÉ ICING

The cake must be completely cold before you ice with glacé icing.

PREPARATION TIME: *10 minutes*
COOKING TIME: *2–3 minutes*
MAKES ENOUGH TO COVER 1 x 20 cm
CAKE

200 g icing sugar, sifted
1–4 tablespoons water
choice of flavourings:
1) ½ teaspoon vanilla essence
2) 1 teaspoon instant coffee dissolved in 1 tablespoon hot water
3) 30 g chocolate melted and cooled
4) 2–3 tablespoons lemon juice or liqueur

1 Mix icing sugar with water to a thick paste. Add flavouring of your choice.

2 Place in a bowl over hot water. When warm and thick enough to coat the back of a spoon, pour over cakes. (If icing is too thick, add a little more water; if too thin, add a little more icing sugar.)

BUTTERCREAM

This is a very rich, velvety-textured buttercream, ideal for filling and frosting. Any remaining buttercream may be frozen for up to three months.

PREPARATION TIME: *25 minutes*
COOKING TIME: *10 minutes*
MAKES ENOUGH TO FILL 2 x 20 cm
CAKES

4 egg yolks
125 g sugar
100 ml water
250 g unsalted butter
choice of flavourings:
1) 200 g chocolate, melted and cooled
2) 2–4 teaspoons instant coffee dissolved in 2 tablespoons hot water and cooled
3) 2 tablespoons any liqueur
4) 2 teaspoons vanilla essence

1 In a bowl beat the egg yolks lightly until mixed.

2 Heat sugar with water in a pan until dissolved. Bring to the boil and boil until syrup reaches 115°C on a sugar thermometer.

3 Gradually pour hot syrup onto egg yolks, beating constantly, and continue beating until mixture is cool and thick.

4 Cream butter until light and fluffy, and gradually beat into egg mixture. Beat in your choice of flavouring.

44

FRUIT AND CREAM

In very hot weather, chill bowl and beaters. Ensure cream is very cold before beating, as this will prevent cream from curdling.

PREPARATION TIME: *10 minutes*
COOKING TIME: *nil*
MAKES ENOUGH TO FILL AND COVER
1 x 18 cm SPONGE SANDWICH

1 cup cream, chilled
2 teaspoons icing sugar, sifted
choice of flavourings:
1) pulp of 4 passionfruit
2) 1 x 250 g punnet strawberries, washed and hulled
3) apricot jam and 8 apricot halves

1 Whip cream with icing sugar. Add flavouring of your choice.

2 If using passionfruit: combine pulp of three passionfruit with the cream. Use to sandwich sponge cakes together and spread on top. Drizzle over remaining passionfruit pulp for decoration.

3 If using strawberries: slice half the strawberries and combine with half the cream. Use to sandwich sponge cakes together. Decorate top of cake with remaining cream and whole strawberries.

4 If using apricots: combine jam with half the cream. Use to sandwich sponge cakes together. Decorate top of cake with remaining cream and the apricot halves.

Basic Sponge Sandwich

Our no fail sponge is easy to follow and ensures success every time.

PREPARATION TIME: *25 minutes*
COOKING TIME: *15 minutes*
MAKES 1 CAKE

3 eggs, separated
¾ cup caster sugar
1 cup self-raising flour, sifted
3 tablespoons very hot water
½ cup strawberry jam (or any favourite jam)
1 x 300 ml carton thickened cream, whipped
2 tablespoons icing sugar

1 Preheat oven to 180°C. Grease and

flour two 20 cm sandwich cake tins.

2 Place egg whites in a clean, dry bowl. Beat until stiff peaks form. Gradually beat in sugar. Beat until thick and glossy.

3 Fold through egg yolks then flour and water.

4 Divide mixture evenly between prepared tins. Bake for 10–15 minutes or until cake springs back when touched.

5 Remove from tins. Cool on a tea-towel placed on a cake rack. When cool, spread with jam then cream. Sandwich layers together. Decorate top of cake with sifted icing sugar.

Variations

1 Chocolate Sponge: replace 1 cup self-raising flour with ¾ cup self-raising flour, sifted with ¼ cup cocoa; replace 3 tablespoons water with 3 tablespoons boiling milk.

2 Coffee Sponge: sift 2 teaspoons instant coffee with the self-raising flour.

3 Lemon Sponge: add 2 teaspoons grated rind with the sugar — ice with lemon icing.

4 Orange Sponge: add 2 teaspoons grated rind with the sugar. Fill with orange liqueur flavoured cream, ice with orange flavoured glacé icing and decorate with orange segments.

5 Nut Sponge: fold in ¼ cup finely ground almonds, hazelnuts, walnuts or pecans. Fill sponge with coffee-flavoured cream.

Do not mix cakes in blenders or processors unless specified. Use a small electric mixer for best results. Remember to keep scraping the mixture from the sides of the bowl for even mixing.

Basic Sponge Sandwich

Strawberry Cake

For a professional finish, brush strawberries used for decoration with a little warmed redcurrant jelly or sieved strawberry jam. This gives an attractive sheen and intensifies the colour of the berries.

PREPARATION TIME: *1 hour*
COOKING TIME: *30 minutes*
MAKES 1 CAKE

1 cup caster sugar 250g /30s
2 teaspoons grated lemon rind
5 egg yolks
¼ cup boiling water
2 tablespoons lemon juice
1¼ cups self-raising flour 50s
5 egg whites
1½ cups cream
½ teaspoon vanilla essence
1 tablespoon icing sugar
2 x 250 g punnets strawberries, washed and hulled

1 Preheat oven to 180°C. Grease and flour two 20 cm square cake tins.

2 Stir together sugar and lemon rind. Beat egg yolks until light, then gradually beat in sugar. When very thick and creamy, stir in boiling water and lemon juice.

3 Sift flour twice, then sift over top of egg yolk mixture. Fold in lightly but thoroughly.

4 Whip egg whites until thick and fold in lightly. Divide mixture evenly between tins. Bake for 30 minutes, or until top springs back when touched. Turn out onto wire racks to cool.

5 Whip cream with vanilla and icing sugar until stiff. Chop most of the strawberries and fold through three-quarters of the cream. Save remaining cream and some whole strawberries for decoration.

6 With a sharp knife, carefully cut both cakes through the centre making four layers. Sandwich layers together with strawberry cream. Pipe reserved cream in a trellis pattern over the top, and decorate with whole strawberries.

Layered Sponge

Be careful not to overbeat chocolate cream mixture or it will curdle. Beat just until stiff and thick.
When time is limited, use a commercial sponge or madeira cake, instead of making your own.

PREPARATION TIME: *30 minutes plus 24 hours chilling time*
COOKING TIME: *5 minutes*
MAKES 1 CAKE

90 g milk chocolate, broken in pieces
60 g dark chocolate
2½ cups cream
1 Génoise sponge cooked in deep round
20 cm cake tin
brandy for sprinkling
60 g dark chocolate for decorating

1 Heat chocolate and cream in a pan, stirring constantly until mixture comes to the boil. Remove from heat immediately and cool. Put in the refrigerator for 24 hours.

2 Cut sponge carefully into three layers. Sprinkle each layer with brandy.

3 Divide chocolate cream into three portions and beat each until stiff (if all the cream is beaten together it will not thicken). Fill cake with two-thirds of the cream. Use the rest to spread over the cake. Decorate with chocolate curls of dark chocolate.

Using a long-bladed, serrated knife, cut sponge carefully in three layers.

Layered Sponge and Cornflour Sponge

Génoise Sponge

Cornflour Sponge

This recipe includes a little cornflour, which gives the sponge a finer texture.

PREPARATION TIME: *25 minutes*
COOKING TIME: *20 minutes*
MAKES 1 CAKE

3 eggs
125 g caster sugar
⅓ cup cornflour
½ cup plain flour
1½ teaspoons baking powder
2 tablespoons hot water
1 teaspoon melted butter

1 Preheat oven to 180°C. Grease and flour two 20 cm sandwich tins.

2 Place egg whites in a clean, dry bowl. Beat until stiff peaks form. Gradually add sugar. Beat until thick and glossy.

3 Fold in egg yolks and combine. Sift together cornflour, flour and baking powder three times. Gently fold into mixture with water and melted butter. Divide mixture evenly between prepared tins.

4 Bake for 15–20 minutes or until cake springs back when touched.

5 Remove from tins. Cool on a tea-towel placed on a cake rack. When cool sandwich together with filling of your choice.

Génoise Sponge

This French sponge does not require the eggs to be separated.

PREPARATION TIME: *25 minutes*
COOKING TIME: *15 minutes*
MAKES 2 x 20 cm CAKES

4 eggs
125 g caster sugar
125 g plain flour, sifted
60 g butter, melted

1 Preheat oven to 180°C. Grease and flour two 20 cm sandwich tins.

2 Place eggs and sugar into a mixer and beat on high speed for 10 minutes. Mixture should be very pale, frothy and quite thick in consistency.

3 Remove beaters. Using a metal spoon fold in sifted flour and melted butter until just combined.

4 Divide mixture evenly between prepared tins. Bake for 20–25 minutes or until cake springs back when touched. Remove from tins. Cool on a tea-towel placed on a cake rack.

5 When cold, fill with cream and sprinkle with icing sugar.

Sunshine Lemon Torte

The zesty and refreshing flavour of lemon combines delightfully with this melt-in-the-mouth sponge. Serve this one for a special occasion.

PREPARATION TIME: *1 hour*
COOKING TIME: *15 minutes*
MAKES 1 CAKE

4 eggs
125 g caster sugar
125 g self-raising flour
60 g butter, melted
125 g lemon-flavoured spread
300 ml cream, whipped
LEMON ICING
4 cups icing sugar, sifted
1 teaspoon butter, softened
3 tablespoons lemon juice
1 tablespoon hot water
1–2 lemons, shredded coconut or crystallised flowers, for decoration

1 Preheat oven to 180°C. Grease and flour two 18 cm sandwich tins.

2 Place whole eggs and sugar in a large mixer bowl. Beat on medium speed for 10 minutes until thick and pale. Bubbles in the mixture will be small and fine, and mixture should form a ribbon when beaters are lifted.

3 Sift flour directly over egg mixture. Using a metal spoon, fold in flour until just combined. Add butter and fold in the same way.

4 Divide mixture evenly between prepared tins. Bake for 10–15 minutes until cake springs back when touched. Turn out onto a cake rack to cool. Using a sharp knife, cut sponges horizontally in half.

5 Place first cake layer on a serving platter. Cover with lemon spread. Top with another cake layer. Spread with whipped cream. Continue spreading cake layers with lemon spread and cream until all layers are used.

6 To prepare icing: combine icing sugar with butter, lemon juice and hot water. Beat well to a smooth consistency. Spread icing over entire cake and decorate as desired.

Step 1 Beat whole eggs and sugar on a medium speed for 10 minutes (mixture should form a ribbon when beaters are lifted).

Step 2 Using a metal spoon, fold in flour until just combined.

Step 3 Using a sharp knife, cut sponges horizontally in half.

Step 4 Place first layer on serving plate. Cover with lemon spread. Top with another cake layer, spread with cream. Repeat layers.

Lemon Curd or Lemon Spread is a delicious lemon preserve made from lemon, butter, sugar and eggs. It is ideal for filling tarts, pies and pastries.

Pecan Roulade

Flavour cream with a little coffee liqueur and fold through ½ cup grated chocolate, for a delicious filling.

PREPARATION TIME: *50 minutes*
COOKING TIME: *20 minutes*
MAKES 1 ROLL

185 g pecans
1 teaspoon baking powder
6 eggs, separated
⅔ cup sugar
1 tablespoon caster sugar
300 ml cream
1 teaspoon vanilla essence
1 tablespoon icing sugar
extra pecans for decoration

1 Preheat oven to 180°C. Grease a 30 x 25 cm Swiss roll tin, line and grease paper.

2 In a food processor, grind nuts until finely chopped. Transfer to a large bowl and stir through baking powder. Place egg yolks and ½ cup sugar into processor. Process until very thick and pale. Add to chopped pecans.

3 Using an electric mixer, beat egg whites until stiff. Beat in remaining sugar and continue beating until white and glossy. Fold one-third of the whites into pecan mixture; then fold in remaining whites.

4 Pour into prepared tin. Bake for 15–20 minutes until cake springs back when touched. Cool 5 minutes then turn out onto paper sprinkled with caster sugar. Remove tin and greased paper carefully. Roll up cake in paper from short end. Cool.

5 Using a mixer, whip cream and vanilla to form soft peaks. Add icing sugar and continue beating until stiff. Reserve one-third of the cream for decoration. Unroll cake and fill with remaining cream. Reroll cake and lift onto a serving plate.

6 Decorate cake with remaining cream and top with pecans to serve.

Step 1 Grind pecans until finely chopped. Transfer to large bowl and stir through baking powder.

Step 2 Beat egg whites until stiff. Beat in remaining sugar until glossy.

Step 3 Roll up cake in paper from short end (placing roulade on a clean tea towel helps with this step).

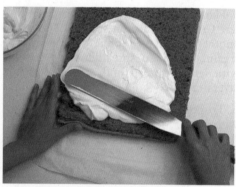

Step 4 Unroll cake and fill with sweetened cream. Reroll cake and lift onto serving plate.

Pecan Roulade and Powder Puffs

Powder Puffs

If you don't have a piping bag, spoon out even-size rounds with a teaspoon.

PREPARATION TIME: *40 minutes*
COOKING TIME: *6 minutes per batch*
MAKES ABOUT 15

2 eggs
½ cup caster sugar
½ cup self-raising flour
1 tablespoon cornflour
1 tablespoon hot water
sweetened whipped cream
sifted icing sugar

1 Preheat oven to 160°C and sprinkle two oven trays with cornflour.

2 Separate eggs. Beat egg whites until soft peaks form. Gradually add sugar, beating well after each addition. Add egg yolks and continue beating until pale, thick and glossy. Sift flour and cornflour three times. Lightly fold flours and hot water through egg mixture with a metal spoon.

3 Using a piping bag with a 1 cm nozzle, form mixture into small rounds on prepared trays. Bake for six minutes. Puffs should be quite pale and just browning around the edges. Carefully lift onto a wire rack and leave until cold.

4 Join together in pairs with sweetened whipped cream and lightly dust with sifted icing sugar.

Ginger Sponge and Chocolate Layer Sponge

Ginger Sponge

As a variation for our Ginger Sponge flavour cream with honey and toasted coconut.

PREPARATION TIME: *30 minutes*
COOKING TIME: *25 minutes*
MAKES 1 CAKE

3 eggs, separated
4 tablespoons caster sugar
4½ tablespoons arrowroot
2 tablespoons plain flour
1 teaspoon bicarbonate of soda
2 teaspoons cream of tartar
1 teaspoon cinnamon
1½ teaspoons cocoa
2 teaspoons powdered ginger
2 teaspoons golden syrup
whipped cream and icing sugar to fill and decorate

1 Preheat oven to 180°C. Grease and flour two 18 cm sandwich cake tins.

2 Place egg whites in a clean, dry bowl. Beat until stiff peaks form. Gradually add sugar. Beat until thick and glossy.

3 Fold in egg yolks and combine. Fold in well sifted dry ingredients and warmed golden syrup.

4 Divide mixture evenly between prepared tins. Bake for 20–25 minutes or until cake springs back when touched. Remove from tins. Cool on a tea-towel placed on a cake rack.

5 When cold, fill with cream and sprinkle with icing sugar.

To fill Ginger Sponge with cream, spread an even layer of cream over sponge, pipe remaining cream around edge. Carefully top with sponge. Dust with icing sugar to serve.

Chocolate Layer Sponge

Try adding coffee liqueur to the cream filling and glacé icing for a mocha layer sponge.

PREPARATION TIME: *40 minutes plus 30 minutes chilling time*
COOKING TIME: *20 minutes*
MAKES 1 CAKE

4 eggs
1 cup caster sugar
30 g butter
2½ tablespoons cocoa
4 tablespoons boiling water
1¼ cups self-raising flour, sifted
walnut halves to garnish
CREAM FILLING
1 cup cream
1 tablespoon cocoa
1 tablespoon caster sugar
GLACÉ ICING
1 cup icing sugar
2 tablespoons cocoa
1 tablespoon water
vanilla essence to taste

1 Preheat oven to 180°C. Grease and flour two 20 cm sandwich tins.

2 Beat whole eggs and sugar until pale, glossy and thick.

3 Add butter and cocoa to boiling water, stirring until combined. Sift flour over surface of egg mixture and fold in lightly with cocoa mixture.

4 Divide mixture evenly between prepared tins. Bake for 15–20 minutes or until cake springs back when touched. Turn out onto a cake rack to cool. Split each sponge layer in half.

5 To prepare filling: put cream in a bowl and sprinkle over cocoa and sugar. Chill for at least 30 minutes. Whip until thick. Join cake layers together with filling.

6 To prepare icing: sift together icing sugar and cocoa in a pan. Combine with water and vanilla. Heat very carefully, stirring constantly until mixture becomes thin and smooth. Pour over sponge, spreading with a warm palette knife.

It was not until the eighteenth century that china teacups and saucers were introduced to Britain. By the end of the eighteenth century, tea drinking was widespread, very much helping the growth of the ceramic industry.

Mocha is a coffee bean originally grown in Mocha, Arabia. Today we use the term to indicate a dish flavoured with coffee.

CELEBRATION CAKES

CAKE DECORATION for special occasion cakes is not only a great way to celebrate an important event, but it can also be creative and lots of fun. On these pages, we show you how to achieve the look you want to suit the occasion using our step-by-step techniques.

Chocolate Shapes

PREPARATION TIME: *20 minutes*
COOKING TIME: *2 minutes*
MAKES Any number

cooking chocolate

1 Line a flat tray with grease-proof paper and brush lightly with oil.

2 Melt chocolate over hot water until just melted, ensuring chocolate is not overheated and no moisture gets into it.

3 Spread chocolate over oil on paper to form a thin, even coating. Leave in a cool place to set.

4 Using a shaped cutter or a knife, cut chocolate into desired shape. Chill chocolate before lifting off shapes. Store chocolate shapes in a cool, dry place.

Using sharp cutters, cut out desired shapes. Chill before lifting off shapes.

Chocolate Curls

PREPARATION TIME: *20 minutes*
COOKING TIME: *Nil*
MAKES 200 g

1 x 200 g block cooking chocolate

1 Chocolate curls are usually made by shaving off thin layers from the flat side of a block of chocolate with a knife or vegetable peeler. A spokeshave, which is similar to a small wood plane, used by carpenters for trimming the surface of timber, is much easier to use. It glides easily over the chocolate, making fine or thick curls according to the amount of pressure applied. The cheapest spokeshave you can find at your hardware store will do the job.

2 For the more experienced cook: spread a plastic laminate board thinly with melted chocolate. When almost set insert a knife blade under chocolate and pull towards you, making 'professional' curls.

Insert a flat bladed knife over chocolate, hold it at about a 45° angle, pull over chocolate.

Crystallised Flowers

PREPARATION TIME: *15 minutes*
COOKING TIME: *Nil*
MAKES Any quantity

1 egg white
1 cup caster sugar
small fresh flowers eg. violets or small rose buds; alternatively large petals of roses or carnations.

1 Lightly beat an egg white till broken up and slightly frothy. Pour a small amount of caster sugar in a bowl.

2 Using a small paintbrush, lightly coat petals with egg white and immediately sprinkle with sugar or dip in a bowl of sugar, ensuring petals are well coated.

3 Place on a rack to dry. Store in an airtight container till required.

Lightly coat petals with egg white, sprinkle well with sugar.

HOW TO DECORATE THE PERFECT CAKE

Spun Sugar

PREPARATION TIME: *10 minutes*
COOKING TIME: *10 minutes*
MAKES 1 x 20 cm cake

1 cup sugar
½ cup water

1 Combine sugar and water in saucepan, stir constantly over heat without boiling until sugar is dissolved. Bring to the boil, boil rapidly without stirring until light golden brown.

2 Remove from heat, using a metal spoon, drizzle toffee in a thin stream backwards and forwards over lightly oiled trays. When set, break in small pieces, place on cake.

3 Toffee may also be spun over iced cakes by dipping two forks in toffee mixture back to back and pulling toffee in thin strands over cake.

Chocolate Petals

PREPARATION TIME: *20 minutes*
COOKING TIME: *2 minutes*
MAKES Any number

foil
cooking chocolate

1 Cut squares of foil into several pieces of three sizes: 10 cm, 7 cm and 5 cm square. Melt chocolate over hot water until just melted. Remove from heat and cool slightly.

2 Hold a foil square in the palm of one hand. With a palette knife, spoon or paintbrush, thinly spread melted chocolate onto foil.

3 While chocolate is still soft, lift your fingers under the foil to slightly bend petal into natural shape. Stand until set. Repeat with remaining chocolate.

4 Carefully peel foil away from chocolate.

1. Drizzle toffee over trays.

1. Brush foil with chocolate, bend into shape.

2. Using two forks, pull toffee into strands.

2. Carefully peel foil away.

Special Occasion Cakes

Let's Celebrate

THESE CAKES ARE MORE THAN JUST CAKES. Extra rich ingredients, rich icings and fillings, and elaborate presentation make them sensational fare for special occasions.

Most of these recipes should be made 1–2 days before serving, to allow flavours to mature. This is a bonus for busy hostesses, who like to prepare as much as possible in advance.

We have also included some Christmas specialities – one of these cakes is bound to become your family's traditional celebration cake. If you like to try something different, bake the Christmas Wreath, an easy cake which is popular in the USA. If you like a light fruit cake, Cherry and Nut Christmas Cake may be just for you.

Doboz Torte

'Gâteau' is the French word for cakes of all types — plain, dessert, and decorated cakes. In many other parts of the world 'gâteau' is regarded as a special occasion cake layered with cream, flavoured with liqueur and interspersed with chocolate, nuts and fruits.

POINTERS FOR PERFECTION

Busy cooks often take advantage of the convenience of a reliable cake mix, spending time on a rich filling and frosting to produce a delicious special occasion cake. Try some of the many cake mix varieties available, choose a basic butter or chocolate base and follow our recipes to produce impressive dessert cakes.

Non-stick baking paper and greaseproof paper are essential for lining tins and for making paper piping bags; fold a 25.5 cm square of greaseproof paper diagonally in half, then roll into a cone shape. Fold the points inwards to secure them. Snip off the tip of the bag and use with or without a nozzle.

Dessert cakes are best made a day or so before needed, cover with plastic wrap and store in the refrigerator. Cover with cream or frosting and decorate just before serving.

The combination of sweet seasonal fruits and whipped cream gives sumptuous results. Any kind of fresh fruit or soft berry may be used — ensure fruit is of a soft texture for ease of cutting cake. When firmer fruits are used they may need gentle poaching to achieve desired texture.

Chocolate, nuts and crystallised flowers are inspirational in the decoration of cakes. Walnuts, pecan nuts and hazelnuts are popular. Store nuts in refrigerator or freezer to stop rancidity. Chop nuts finely for decoration and ease of cake service. Choose good quality chocolate for grating, chopping, and decorating. Crumbled chocolate flake makes a useful last minute decoration.

When buying dried fruits, choose clean fruit which has no musty smell. The best quality dried fruits are sold as 'dessert' fruit. Fruit may be measured and sprinkled with brandy, rum or sherry. Store covered in advance of cake making.

Almond Date Torte

Dried figs may replace the dates in this recipe for a delicious variation.

PREPARATION TIME: *45 minutes*
COOKING TIME: *40 minutes*
MAKES 1

4 eggs
⅔ cup caster sugar
1⅓ cups ground almonds
1 cup chopped dates
apricot jam
RUM GLAZE
½ cup icing sugar, sifted
1 teaspoon butter
1 teaspoon milk
1 teaspoon rum

1 Preheat oven to 180°C. Grease 2 x 18 cm sandwich tins, line with greaseproof paper and grease paper.

2 Beat eggs. Gradually beat in sugar and continue beating until thick and creamy. Mix together ground almonds and dates and fold in gently.

3 Turn into prepared tins and bake for 35–40 minutes, or until cooked when tested. Remove from tins and leave until next day. Join together with a layer of jam and top with glaze.

4 To prepare glaze: heat all ingredients in a small pan. Stir over gentle heat until butter has melted and ingredients are well mixed. Pour over top of cake and quickly spread with a spatula. Serve with sweetened sour cream on the side.

Doboz Torte

In warm humid weather, store cake in an airtight container in a cool place, to avoid caramel topping becoming soft and sticky. This beautiful special-occasion cake is of Hungarian origin and is made by the sponge method.

PREPARATION TIME: *2 hours*
COOKING TIME: *50 minutes*
MAKES 1 CAKE

1¼ cups plain flour
4 eggs
¾ cup caster sugar
1 cup crystal sugar

Almond Date Torte

½ *cup water*
BUTTERCREAM
4 egg yolks
1 cup caster sugar
1¼ cups milk
500 g unsalted butter
250 g dark chocolate, melted
over hot water

1 Preheat oven to 180°C. Grease and lightly flour several oven trays.

2 Sift flour into a bowl. Beat eggs and gradually beat in caster sugar. Continue beating until pale, thick and creamy. Fold in flour lightly, and divide mixture into six equal portions.

3 Mark 20 cm circles on oven trays and spread a portion of mixture into each circle. Bake for 5–8 minutes.

4 Trim each round while still on tray, remove to a wire rack and leave until cold. Continue until all layers are cooked. (After each is cooked, the tray must be wiped, re-oiled and floured.

5 Heat sugar and water in a pan over low heat until sugar dissolves. Increase heat and cook rapidly until a rich, brown caramel colour. Take one of the cake rounds and place on an oiled wire cake rack. Pour caramel over and when just about to set, mark into 12 serving portions with an oiled knife. Trim around edge and set aside.

6 To prepare cream: beat egg yolks with half the sugar until thick and creamy. Dissolve rest of sugar in milk. Bring to boiling point, pour onto yolks and stir over gentle heat until mixture coats the back of a spoon. Chill until cool and thickened. Beat butter until soft. Gradually whisk custard into butter with cooled, melted chocolate.

7 Join layers together with some of the buttercream, arranging the caramel covered round on top. Spread the rest of the cream over sides of cake.

Note: if you wish, press grated chocolate over cream-covered sides, or make extra caramel, crush fairly finely and press over cream.

To prevent cream from curdling, chill bowl and beaters and ensure cream is very cold before beating. A balloon whisk gives excellent results when whipping cream. Beat cream until just stiff and thick.

*White Chocolate and
Strawberry Gâteau*

White Chocolate and Strawberry Gâteau

The subtle tastes of white chocolate and strawberries combine to make this gâteau a taste sensation.

PREPARATION TIME: *2 hours*
COOKING TIME: *35 minutes*
MAKES 1 CAKE

*1 x 370 g packet vanilla cake mix
red food colouring*
TOPPING
*2 x 250 g punnets strawberries,
hulled
¼ cup sugar
1 x 7 g sachet plain gelatine
300 ml thickened cream
150 g white chocolate
chocolate petals, optional (see recipe)*

1 Preheat oven to 180°C. Grease a deep 18 cm round cake tin, line base with baking paper and grease paper. Lightly flour.

2 Prepare cake mix following instructions on packet. Divide batter in half.

To create chocolate petals follow the easy recipe on page 55.

Tint one portion pink, using a few drops of red food colouring.

3 Spoon large dollops of each batter alternately into prepared tin. Drag a sharp knife through batters to create a marbled effect.

4 Bake for 30–35 minutes until top springs back when gently pressed. Briefly cool in tin. Turn out onto a wire rack to cool completely. Thinly trim dome of cake to an even level.

5 To prepare topping: purée half the strawberries. Place in a pan with sugar and gelatine. Stir over moderate heat until sugar dissolves. Simmer for two minutes. Cool to room temperature, stirring frequently. Beat cream until stiff. Fold in prepared strawberry mixture.

6 Tape a strip of baking paper around cake to stand about 5 cm above the rim. Reserve ⅓ cup topping. Pour remainder onto cake. Reserve three of the smaller strawberries; gently push remainder into topping. Chill 15 minutes or until topping sets. Remove paper. Smoothly spread reserved topping mixture over the sides of the cake.

7 To prepare chocolate coating: cut a strip of baking paper about 62 x 10 cm. (Strip should be as wide as the cake, including topping, is tall.) Melt white chocolate over simmering water. Spread smoothly over strip, leaving a 2 cm border at each end. Briefly stand until chocolate just begins to set.

8 Quickly lift strip and wrap chocolate around cake. Slightly overlap ends and gently press to sides, smoothing evenly. Stand until set then carefully peel off paper. Prepare chocolate petals if using. Arrange petals decoratively over top of cake. Stand cake at room temperature for about 30 minutes before serving. Decorate top with remaining strawberries, as desired.

Cherry and Nut Christmas Cake

Cherry and Nut Christmas Cake

Unsalted butter may be used in this recipe. Test if cake is cooked by inserting a skewer into the centre of the cake. If the skewer is clean and dry when removed, the cake is cooked. Check the cake halfway through cooking time. If beginning to brown, cover top loosely with foil.

PREPARATION TIME: *1 hour*
COOKING TIME: *2 hours*
MAKES 1 CAKE

250 g butter
1¼ cups caster sugar
few drops almond essence
5 eggs
3 cups self-raising flour, sifted
⅓ cup desiccated coconut
150 ml milk
2 cups chopped red glacé cherries
¼ cup chopped blanched almonds
¼ cup chopped pecans
ICING
4 cups icing sugar, sifted
1 teaspoon butter
3 tablespoons hot water
1 tablespoon lemon juice

1 Preheat oven to 160°C. Grease and line a 23 cm square cake tin.

2 Cream butter and sugar together until light and fluffy. Blend in almond essence. Add eggs one at a time. Beat well after each addition.

3 Fold flour and coconut into creamed mixture alternately with milk, finishing with flour. Mix in cherries and nuts.

4 Pour into prepared tin and bake for 1½–2 hours or until cooked when tested. Cool.

5 To prepare icing: combine all ingredients well. Mix to a stiff paste, adding more water if required. Spread icing over the entire cake. Decorate as desired.

Café Cake

Our spectacular Café Cake is an impressive special occasion cake. Decorate with toffee just before serving.

PREPARATION TIME: *1 hour*
COOKING TIME: *30 minutes*
MAKES 1 CAKE

1 x 370 g packet vanilla cake mix
6 teaspoons instant coffee
1 tablespoon hot water
BUTTERCREAM
250 g unsalted butter
1½ cups icing sugar
2–3 teaspoons instant coffee
1 tablespoon hot water
½ cup chopped walnuts
GARNISH
1½ cups sugar
¼ cup water
vegetable oil
60 g dark chocolate, melted

1 Preheat oven to 180°C. Grease a deep 19 cm square cake tin. Line base with baking paper and grease paper. Lightly flour.

2 Prepare cake mix following packet instructions. Dissolve coffee in hot water and stir into batter. Turn into prepared tin.

3 Bake for 25–30 minutes until top springs back when gently pressed. Briefly cool in tin. Turn out onto a wire rack to cool completely. Split horizontally into two layers.

4 To prepare buttercream: beat butter with icing sugar until creamy. Dissolve coffee in hot water. Cool, then beat into buttercream. Combine ½ cup buttercream with walnuts and fill layers. Spread rest of mixture smoothly over top and sides.

5 Combine sugar and water in pan. Stir constantly over medium heat, without boiling, until sugar is dissolved. Then boil rapidly, uncovered and without stirring, until golden. Crush a sheet of foil and spread smoothly to line a large baking tray. Brush with oil. Pour hot syrup onto tray, quickly tilting to spread toffee thinly. Cool.

6 Break toffee into uniform pieces. Press on sides of cake. Pipe melted chocolate into thin decorative lines over top of cake.

Praline originated in France in the seventeenth century. Named after its creator, the French Comte De Plessis-Praslin, this delicious sweetmeat of toffee and almond is used to flavour desserts, sauces, ices and fillings.

Glacé is the French word for glazed. It is particularly applied to fruits dipped in heavy sugar syrup which hardens when cold, glacé cherries being the most popular. Glacé fruit is often confused with crystallised fruit which are small fruits or pieces of fruit that are cooked and soaked in a sugar syrup. After draining and drying, the fruit has a dry sugary coating and is eaten as a sweet or used for decoration.

Step 1 Split Café Cake horizontally into two layers.

Step 2 Dissolve coffee in hot water, cool, then beat into butter cream.

Step 3 Spread remaining buttercream smoothly over sides and top of cake.

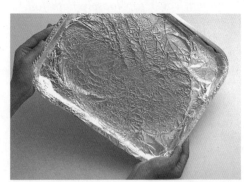

Step 4 Pour hot syrup onto foil-lined tray, quickly tilting to spread toffee thinly. Cool.

Café Cake

Treacles are blends of sugar syrups with the addition of molasses. There are several grades available, from light golden to black in colour, used to enhance the flavour and colour of fruit cakes and desserts.

Pina Colada Roll

This cake tastes delicious served with rum-soaked fruit such as pineapple, strawberries, grapes, tamarillos, melon balls or kiwi fruit.

PREPARATION TIME: *1¼ hours plus 2 hours freezing time*
COOKING TIME: *12 minutes*
MAKES 1 CAKE

⅔ cup plain flour, sifted
¾ teaspoon baking powder
2 eggs
½ cup caster sugar
2 tablespoons water
¾ teaspoon vanilla essence
60 g dark chocolate, melted and slightly cooled
a little sifted icing or caster sugar
1½ tablespoons light rum (optional)
1 litre vanilla ice-cream, slightly softened
1 cup crushed pineapple, well-drained
½ cup coconut cream
1 cup cream, whipped
toasted coconut to decorate

1 Preheat oven to 180°C. Grease and line a 30 x 25 cm Swiss roll tin with grease-proof paper and grease paper.

2 Sift flour and baking powder three times into a bowl. Set aside. Beat eggs until fluffy. Gradually beat in sugar until very thick, about five minutes. Stir in water, vanilla and melted chocolate. Fold in flour mixture.

3 Spread batter in prepared tin. Bake for about 12 minutes until cake springs back when gently pressed.

4 Loosen cake in tin. Invert on a clean tea-towel sprinkled with caster sugar. Peel off paper. Roll up cake in towel from short end and cool completely on a wire rack. Sprinkle unrolled cake with rum, if desired.

5 Stir together ice-cream, pineapple and coconut cream. Spread over cake, then re-roll firmly. Wrap tightly in foil and freeze for 1½ hours or until firm.

6 To decorate: place cake, seam side down, on a serving plate. Spread with whipped cream, swirling slightly. Sprinkle with toasted coconut and return to freezer. Remove 10–15 minutes before serving for easier slicing.

Brandy Snap Torte

Unfilled brandy snaps are readily available from specialty cake and biscuit stores.

PREPARATION TIME: *40 minutes plus overnight chilling time*
COOKING TIME: *20 minutes*
MAKES 1 CAKE

5 eggs, separated
½ cup caster sugar
1 teaspoon vanilla essence
⅔ cup plain flour, sifted
FILLING
185 g unsalted butter, softened
¾ cup cocoa
2 egg yolks
2 cups icing sugar, sifted
½ cup cream
2 teaspoons vanilla essence
1½ cups cream, whipped
6–8 brandy snaps

1 Preheat oven to 180°C. Grease two 23 cm square cake tins, line with grease-proof paper and grease paper.

2 Beat egg whites in a large bowl until soft peaks form. Sprinkle in 3 tablespoons sugar, a tablespoon at a time, beating well after each addition. Continue beating until meringue is stiff and glossy, then fold in vanilla.

3 With same beaters, beat egg yolks and remaining sugar in another bowl until thick and fluffy. Sift flour over the top and fold in, then fold in about a third of the meringue.

4 Fold this mixture into remaining meringue and spoon evenly into prepared tins. Bake for 12–15 minutes or until centres spring back lightly when touched with fingertips. Turn out and allow to cool on wire racks.

5 Cut each cake in half crossways then split the four pieces in two to make eight layers altogether.

6 To prepare filling: melt 60 g butter in the top of a double boiler or a bowl set over simmering water. Add cocoa and mix well. Remove from heat, and beat in remaining butter and egg yolks. Add icing sugar alternately with cream, beating well between each addition. Stir in vanilla. Chill for 10 minutes before using.

7 Trim any crusts from cake and make sure layers are even in size. Sandwich layers together with filling, using a slightly rounded ¼ cup of filling between each layer. Smooth remaining filling over sides and top. Chill for several hours or overnight.

8 When ready to serve, pipe cream into both ends of brandy snaps and arrange on top of torte. Pipe remaining cream in small rosettes around base and top edge.

Almond Cheesecake

If you invert the base of a springform tin and insert it upside down, it makes a flat base which is easier to remove.

PREPARATION TIME: *1 hour plus 1 hour chilling time*
COOKING TIME: *1 hour*
MAKES 1 CAKE

1 cup crushed gingernut biscuits
½ cup ground almonds
1¼ cups sugar
60 g butter, melted
250 g ricotta cheese

500 g cream cheese softened and cut into cubes
1 teaspoon almond essence
3 eggs
¼ cup plain flour
whipped cream and fresh fruit to serve

1 Preheat oven to 180°C. Line base of a deep 23 cm springform tin with greaseproof paper and grease paper.

2 Combine biscuit crumbs, almonds and ¼ cup sugar. Stir in melted butter until moistened. Press into base and up sides of prepared tin.

3 Bake for 10 minutes. Remove from oven and cool.

4 In a large bowl with an electric mixer, beat ricotta cheese until smooth. Add cream cheese, remaining 1 cup sugar and essence. Beat well until blended. Beat in eggs, one at a time. Stir in flour until blended.

5 Pour filling into cooled crust. Bake for 45–50 minutes, or until filling is set and firm to the touch.

6 Cool in tin 1 hour. Gently release sides of tin and remove cheesecake. Chill well prior to cutting. Top with whipped cream and fresh fruit to serve.

Pina Colada Roll and Brandy Snap Torte

Almond Cheesecake, Mango Coconut Terrine and Sicilian Party Cake

Mango and Coconut Terrine

When in season fresh mangoes may be used in our impressive Mango and Coconut Terrine.

PREPARATION TIME: *2 hours plus several hours standing time*
COOKING TIME: *40 minutes*
MAKES 1 CAKE

1 x 340 g packet coconut or plain cake mix
FILLING
2 teaspoons plain gelatine
2 tablespoons water
1 x 425 g can mangoes, drained
1 tablespoon white rum
1 x 310 g packet continental cheesecake dessert mix (see Note)
¾ cup coconut milk
¼ cup sieved apricot jam, warmed
toasted shredded coconut to garnish
MANGO RUM COULIS *(optional)*
1 x 425 g can mangoes, drained
2 tablespoons white rum
¼ cup thickened cream (optional)

1 Preheat oven to 180°C. Grease and line a 21 x 11 x 6 cm loaf tin with baking paper. Choose a tin with straight, not rounded corners. Grease and flour paper.

2 Prepare cake mix following packet instructions. Pour into prepared tin and bake for 35–40 minutes until a skewer inserted in the centre comes out clean. Briefly cool in tin. Turn out onto a wire rack to cool completely.

3 Line base and sides of the clean dry loaf tin with baking paper. Thinly trim all sides of cake to remove crusts and level the top. Cut horizontally into five equal slices. Reserve one slice; use remainder to line base and sides of prepared tin, cutting cake as needed to fit snugly. Set aside.

4 To prepare filling: soften gelatine in the water, stirring over hot water until dissolved. Cool slightly. Purée mangoes with rum. Reserve 2 tablespoons purée for glaze. Stir gelatine into remaining purée. Chill, stirring frequently until filling just begins to set.

5 In a bowl combine the filling sachet from cheesecake mix with coconut milk. Beat with an electric mixer at medium speed for three minutes until thick and creamy. Spoon half the mixture into prepared tin. Carefully spread mango filling over cheese layer. Chill until firm.

6 Top with remaining cheese mixture. Carefully press reserved cake slice over top, trimming if needed to fit flush with all sides. Chill several hours until firm.

7 To serve: unmould terrine onto an attractive serving plate. Stir together warm jam and reserved mango purée. Brush mixture over top and sides of the cake to glaze. Sprinkle with coconut to garnish. May be served with Mango Rum Coulis, if desired.

8 To prepare coulis: purée mangoes with rum. Cover and keep chilled until ready to serve. Spoon coulis onto dessert plates and top with slices of terrine. Thinly drizzle cream, if desired, over coulis. Draw a skewer through to create a marble effect. Serve at once.

Note: reserve the biscuit base sachet for another use.

Christmas Wreath

Christmas Wreath

Our American Christmas Wreath may be brushed with brandy or rum while still hot for a rich flavour.

PREPARATION TIME: *50 minutes*
COOKING TIME: *1½ hours*
MAKES 1 CAKE

250 g dessert dates
125 g glacé pineapple
125 g glacé apricots
125 g red glacé cherries
125 g green glacé cherries
125 g whole blanched almonds
250 g shelled Brazil nuts
125 g seeded raisins
125 g halved stoned prunes
2 eggs
½ cup brown sugar
1 teaspoon vanilla essence
2 tablespoons rum
90 g butter, softened
½ cup plain flour
½ teaspoon baking powder

1 Preheat oven to 150°C. Grease a 20 cm ring tin and line the base with greaseproof paper and grease paper.

2 Stone dates, then chop pineapple and apricots into fairly large pieces. Leave remaining fruits and nuts whole. Mix all fruits and nuts, reserving ½ cup combined nuts and glacé fruits for topping.

3 Beat eggs until light and fluffy. Add sugar, vanilla essence, rum and butter. Continue beating until well blended. Sift flour with baking powder three times. Add to mixture with fruit and nuts. Combine thoroughly.

4 Spoon mixture evenly into prepared tin. Arrange reserved ½ cup fruit and nuts over the top, pressing down gently. Bake for about 1½ hours, or until cake is firm to touch. Cool for 10 minutes in the tin before turning out. Store in an airtight container wrapped in greaseproof paper.

Marsala is a fortified wine from Sicily and appears in many dishes from Italy. Its rich delicious flavour features in the classic Zabaglione, but it can also be used to enhance veal and beef dishes. Surprisingly, it can be used to flavour a rich tomato sauce, while it is indispensable in dessert cookery.

2 In a pan combine almonds, dried fruits, raisins and orange juice. Heat until boiling, stirring constantly. Add brandy. Stand pan in a sink of cold water to cool quickly (stir occasionally).

3 In a large mixing bowl, place flours, butter, spices, eggs and treacle. Thoroughly beat with an electric mixer until well blended. Stir in cooled fruit mixture.

4 Turn into prepared tin, smoothing the surface. Bake for 1½ hours or until cooked and firm to touch (loosely cover with foil after the first 45 minutes). Cool in tin on a wire rack.

5 Remove from tin and wrap in plastic wrap, foil or greaseproof paper. Store airtight in a cool, dry, dark place for up to one month before serving.

Note: you may prefer to use your own mix of dried fruits.

Rich Wholemeal Fruit Cake

To decorate your cake, place it upside down on a 25 cm cake board. Brush top with warmed apricot jam and liberally sprinkle with desiccated coconut. Tie a thick red ribbon around outside of cake, secure at the back with pins or sticky tape and remove before cutting. Decorate with holly sprigs and red curling ribbon. Add festive candles, if desired.

PREPARATION TIME: *1 hour*
COOKING TIME: *1¾ hours*
MAKES 1 CAKE

1 cup blanched almonds, chopped
500 g mixed dried fruit (see Note)
155 g each of dried pears, peaches and apricots, chopped
1 cup raisins
300 ml orange juice
½ cup brandy
1¼ cups wholemeal flour
1 cup plain flour
300 g butter, softened
1 teaspoon each mixed spice and cinnamon
5 eggs, beaten
⅓ cup treacle

1 Preheat oven to 150°C. Line a 23 cm round or square cake tin with a layer of brown paper then a layer of baking paper.

Sicilian Party Cake

Combine marsala with a little milk and brush over cake before frosting for a very moist result.

PREPARATION TIME: *1½ hours plus 5½ hours chilling time*
COOKING TIME: *35 minutes*
MAKES 1 CAKE

3 eggs, separated
¼ cup caster sugar
2 tablespoons water
1 tablespoon lemon juice
2 teaspoons grated orange rind
1 cup self-raising flour
¼ teaspoon cream of tartar
3 tablespoons icing sugar, sifted
FILLING
250 g ricotta cheese
1 tablespoon caster sugar
1 tablespoon sour cream
5 teaspoons marsala
2 teaspoons grated orange rind
⅓ cup mixture finely chopped glacé fruits and finely chopped toasted almonds
2 tablespoons coarsely grated dark chocolate
marsala (optional)
FROSTING
125 g dark chocolate
125 g butter, softened
1½ cups icing sugar sifted

1 Preheat oven to 180°C. Grease and flour a 23 x 12 cm loaf tin.

2 Beat together egg yolks and caster sugar until thick and creamy. Beat in water, lemon juice and grated rind. Sift flour twice and gradually fold in. Beat egg whites with cream of tartar until soft peaks form. Gradually beat in icing sugar, beating until stiff.

3 Fold into yolk mixture, turn into prepared tin and bake for 35 minutes, or until done when tested. Turn out and leave to cool.

4 To prepare filling: push ricotta cheese through a coarse sieve. Beat in sugar, sour cream, marsala and orange rind. Mix in glacé fruits, almonds and chocolate. Chill for one hour.

5 Split cake horizontally into three layers. Spread some filling on one layer, top with the second, spread rest of filling mixture over this and top with the third layer. Press down gently, sprinkle lightly with marsala, if you wish, chill for four hours.

6 To prepare frosting: melt chocolate over hot water. Beat in soft butter. Gradually beat in icing sugar. Continue beating until smooth. Cover top and sides of cake with frosting. Chill again, cut in slices and serve with whipped cream.

Rich Wholemeal Fruit Cake

Ricotta is a soft unripened curd style cheese made from cow's milk or sheep's milk. It is best used within a few days of purchase. To store ricotta, wrap closely with plastic wrap and store in the refrigerator. Ricotta is used in both sweet and savoury foods.

Biscuits

Only the Best

Biscuits come in all styles, shapes and sizes — they can be soft or crispy, plain or iced, shaped, piped or rolled. No matter what size, shape or style you go for, biscuits are always a winner when it comes to snacks, school lunches, and morning and afternoon teas. Anyone who has children knows that biscuit jars need to be bottomless. There's nothing quite so satisfying as the heavenly smell of biscuits fresh baked from your own oven. Whether your penchant is Ginger Spice, Coconut Wafers or Florentines, you will find an inspiring selection of biscuits here.

From top left: Carrot and Raisin Rounds, Finnish Chestnut Fingers (p. 77), Coconut Wafers, Ginger Spice Biscuits (p. 72)   71

To shred coconut meat use a vegetable peeler or small sharp knife to peel the brown outer skin, and then grate with a metal grater or use a processor fitted with a metal blade.

POINTERS FOR PERFECTION

Biscuits usually have a crunchy crisp texture and are shaped individually before cooking.

Most recipes will require flat, small oven trays or slides that should be well greased. Grease biscuit trays with polyunsaturated oil — butter may cause biscuits to stick to the tray. It is most important that biscuits be a uniform size — they both look better and cook evenly. It only takes seconds to scoop mixture into a measuring spoon to obtain the correct quantity before placing on the oven trays.

Minimise kneading and handling the biscuit dough — otherwise dough will toughen.

Biscuits are generally cooked when they turn a light golden brown. Remove from oven, stand 2 minutes, gently loosen from tray using a palette knife and leave on the tray till quite cold. This will crisp the biscuits. Store in an airtight container immediately. Avoid storing different varieties of biscuits together as they absorb flavours and moisture from each other.

Plain biscuits can be sliced or, just before serving, dusted with icing sugar or a little jam.

Ginger Spice Biscuits

These traditional spice biscuits are perfect as Christmas treats. Use a tree-shaped biscuit cutter and decorate with glacé cherries. Use cinnamon if cardamom is unavailable.

PREPARATION TIME: *20 minutes*
COOKING TIME: *15 minutes*
MAKES ABOUT 40

250 g butter
1 cup brown sugar
1 egg yolk
3 cups plain flour
1 tablespoon ground ginger
1 teaspoon ground cardamom or cinnamon

1 Preheat oven to 225°C and grease oven trays.

2 Cream butter and sugar until light and fluffy. Beat in egg yolk and mix well. Add sifted flour and spices to mixture and combine to form a stiff dough.

3 Roll out on a lightly floured board until 1 cm thick. Cut into desired shape with floured cutters. Arrange on prepared trays and bake for 12–15 minutes.

4 Cool on tray. Decorate biscuits with glacé icing and sweets if desired.

Coconut Wafers

Dip biscuits in melted chocolate and serve with coffee as an after dinner treat.

PREPARATION TIME: *30 minutes*
COOKING TIME: *10 minutes per batch*
MAKES ABOUT 50

3 eggs
1 cup sugar
2 tablespoons melted butter
1 teaspoon vanilla
1 cup shredded coconut
2 cups quick-cooking rolled oats

1 Preheat oven to 180°C. Line baking trays with greaseproof paper and grease paper.

2 Beat eggs until foamy, then gradually beat in sugar until mixture is thick. Fold in remaining ingredients.

3 Place half teaspoonfuls of mixture on prepared trays, spacing biscuits about 2.5 cm apart. Bake for 10 minutes, or until edges are just lightly browned.

4 Lift paper from trays and cool biscuits for a few minutes, until they are easy to remove with a spatula. Finish cooling on wire racks.

Suncoast Munchies

Drizzle a little melted chocolate over baked munchies.

PREPARATION TIME: *30 minutes*
COOKING TIME: *12 minutes per batch*
MAKES ABOUT 40

125 g butter, softened
⅔ cup brown sugar
grated zest of 1 orange
1 tablespoon orange juice
1 egg
⅓ cup chopped macadamia nuts
⅓ cup dark choc bits
⅓ cup chopped, drained preserved ginger
¾ cup self-raising flour
½ teaspoon bicarbonate of soda
1 cup rolled oats

1 Preheat oven to 200°C and grease baking trays.

2 In a bowl, cream together butter and sugar. Add orange zest and juice. Beat in egg. Stir in nuts, choc bits and ginger.

3 Sift together flour and bicarbonate of soda. Stir into mixture until combined. Fold in oats.

4 Drop teaspoonfuls of dough onto prepared trays and bake for 10–12 minutes. Cool completely on trays.

Cereal Crunchies

As a variation, you can also press biscuit mixture into an oiled 20 cm square cake tin and top with melted chocolate, before cutting into small squares.

PREPARATION TIME: *20 minutes*
COOKING TIME: *5 minutes*
MAKES ABOUT 24

3 cups breakfast cereal, e.g. Rice Krispies
or Cornflakes
1 cup peanuts
¾ cup light corn syrup or golden syrup
¼ cup sugar
½ cup peanut butter
1 teaspoon vanilla essence
sesame seeds or shredded coconut for
coating (optional)

1 In a large bowl, combine cereal and nuts. Heat together syrup and sugar, stirring until sugar melts. Remove from heat. Blend in peanut butter and vanilla. Pour over cereal and mix well.

2 Shape large spoonfuls into balls and arrange on oiled greaseproof paper. Chill in refrigerator for 10 minutes, remove and press firmly into rounds.

3 Roll balls while still sticky in sesame seeds or coconut. Chill again in refrigerator to set.

In the nineteenth century many types of containers were used to store foods. Sugar and flour were kept in wooden tubs while salt and spices were stored in glazed earthenware jars. Tea and biscuits were stored in tins, not only to keep them fresh but to keep rodents at bay.

Suncoast Munchies

Store biscuits in an airtight container. In very humid weather, add a few grains of rice to the biscuit barrel to keep biscuits fresh.

Florentines

For extra delicious colourful florentines, use chopped mixed glacé fruit instead of mixed peel.

PREPARATION TIME: *30 minutes*
COOKING TIME: *5 minutes plus 10 minutes per batch*
MAKES 24

1 cup slivered blanched almonds
¾ cup chopped mixed peel
⅓ cup plain flour
60 g butter
½ cup cream
½ cup caster sugar
1 cup dark chocolate chips or 125 g dark chocolate, melted

1 Preheat oven to 180°C. Grease and flour two baking trays.

2 Combine almonds, peel and flour; set aside.

3 In a heavy-based pan, combine butter, cream and sugar. Heat to boiling. Remove from heat and stir in fruit-nut mixture.

4 Place tablespoonfuls of batter at least 8 cm apart on prepared trays. Bake for 10 minutes until golden brown. Cool on tray before removing to wire racks to cool completely.

5 Brush melted chocolate over base of biscuits. When nearly set, mark chocolate with wavy lines using a fork. Store in a cool, dry place.

Sour Cream Cookies

These cookies may be spread with lemon icing if desired.

PREPARATION TIME: *30 minutes*
COOKING TIME: *10 minutes per batch*
MAKES ABOUT 50

185 g unsalted butter, softened
1½ cups sugar
2 eggs, beaten
2½ cups plain flour, sifted
½ teaspoon bicarbonate of soda
⅓ cup sour cream

1 Preheat oven to 180°C and grease baking trays.

2 Cream butter and sugar until light and fluffy. Beat in eggs and mix well.

3 Sift flour with soda three times. Stir into creamed mixture alternately with sour cream, mixing well after each addition.

4 Place teaspoonfuls of batter on prepared trays, leaving room for spreading. Bake for about 10 minutes, or until cookies are crisp and pale golden. Cool five minutes on trays, then remove to wire racks to finish cooling.

(left) Florentines (right) Sour Cream Cookies

Chocolate Snowdrops

For a spicy coating combine extra icing sugar with a little ground cinnamon, nutmeg or ginger.

PREPARATION TIME: *30 minutes*
COOKING TIME: *20 minutes per batch*
MAKES ABOUT 30

125 g butter, softened
3 tablespoons icing sugar, sifted
⅔ cup plain flour
⅓ cup cocoa
1 cup finely chopped almonds
extra sifted icing sugar to coat cookies

1 Preheat oven to 150°C. For this recipe use ungreased oven trays.

2 Cream butter and icing sugar until light and fluffy. Add sifted flour and cocoa and mix well. Fold in almonds. Chill until firm enough to handle.

3 Roll a teaspoonful of dough at a time into marble-size balls. Arrange balls on trays, spacing them about 5 cm apart.

4 Bake for 20 minutes or until firm. Carefully remove from baking trays. Roll in icing sugar while still warm. Finish cooling on wire racks. Store in layers (with greaseproof paper between) in an airtight container.

Grandfather's Gingernuts

These biscuits are quite irresistible and always a firm favourite.

PREPARATION TIME: *20 minutes*
COOKING TIME: *15 minutes per batch*
MAKES ABOUT 48

125 g butter
¼ cup golden syrup
2 cups plain flour
3 teaspoons ground ginger
1 teaspoon bicarbonate of soda
4 tablespoons sugar
1 egg

1 Preheat oven to 180°C and grease oven trays.

2 In a small pan, stir together butter and golden syrup until melted.

3 Sift together flour, ginger and soda in a mixing bowl. Stir in sugar. Add syrup mixture and egg. Beat with a wooden spoon until combined.

4 Roll dough into small balls. Arrange on prepared trays. Flatten slightly with the base of a glass covered with plastic wrap.

5 Bake for 12–15 minutes until firm and golden. Cool slightly on tray. Remove to a wire rack to cool completely.

Butter and golden syrup may be melted for 30 seconds on high power (100%) in the microwave.

Coffee houses first began to appear in England in the early 17th century. They soon developed into exclusive clubs, whereas on the Continent coffee houses, or cafés, were frequented by the ordinary folk. Marseilles and Paris were the first cities to open cafés. They proved so popular that Vienna soon followed suit.

Chocolate Snowdrops

Grandfather's Gingernuts

Cheese and Jelly Shortbreads

Cheese and Jelly Shortbreads

Ensure that no more than ¼ teaspoon of redcurrant jelly is placed on each biscuit, since extra will ooze out during cooking and burn on the oven trays. A little raspberry or strawberry jam is delicious when redcurrant is unavailable.

PREPARATION TIME: *30 minutes plus*
1 hour chilling time
COOKING TIME: *25 minutes per batch*
MAKES ABOUT 24

75 g butter
125 g matured cheddar cheese, shredded
1 cup plain flour
1 egg yolk
1 tablespoon icy water
¼ cup redcurrant jelly

1 Preheat oven to 170°C. For this recipe use ungreased oven trays.

2 Rub butter and cheese into flour until mixture resembles fine breadcrumbs. Blend egg yolk and water and mix into dry ingredients, adding more water, if needed, to make a stiff dough.

3 Knead dough on lightly floured surface until smooth. Wrap in plastic and chill for 1 hour. Roll out dough to 3 mm thickness. Cut into rounds with a floured, 4.5 cm cutter. With a sharp paring knife, cut a small X in the centre of half the rounds, cutting through pastry.

4 Place rounds without an X on trays. Top each with ¼ teaspoon of jelly. Top with marked rounds and press edges together to seal.

5 Bake for 25 minutes until set and lightly browned. Serve warm or at room temperature.

Spicy Pepper Nuts

These biscuits store well in an airtight container for up to one week.

PREPARATION TIME: *30 minutes plus*
overnight chilling time
COOKING TIME: *15 minutes per batch*
MAKES ABOUT 30

⅓ cup treacle or golden syrup
60 g butter
1 egg, beaten

Redcurrant jelly is a very handy ingredient to have in your store cupboard. It can be used to flavour sweet and savoury dishes and is delicious when melted and usd to glaze fruit tarts. It also adds that special piquancy to the classic Cumberland Sauce.

2 cups plain flour
¼ cup sugar
¾ teaspoon bicarbonate of soda
¾ teaspoon cinnamon
¼ teaspoon ground cloves
¼ teaspoon nutmeg
pinch freshly ground black pepper
sifted icing sugar for rolling

1 Preheat oven to 180°C and grease oven trays.

2 In a pan, heat together treacle and butter, stirring until butter melts. Cool to room temperature. Stir in egg.

3 Sift together flour, sugar, soda and spices. Stir into treacle mixture, mixing well. Cover and chill several hours or overnight.

4 Shape dough by hand into 25 mm balls. Arrange on prepared trays and bake for 12–14 minutes until firm.

5 Cool on tray. Roll biscuits in icing sugar to coat just before serving. Store in an airtight container.

Finnish Chestnut Fingers

If dough is difficult to roll, chill in the refrigerator for about 30 minutes. This firms the mixture, making it easier to roll. Chestnut fingers may be dipped in lemon glacé icing as an alternative to chocolate.

PREPARATION TIME: *45 minutes*
COOKING TIME: *20 minutes per batch*
MAKES ABOUT 30

60 g butter, softened
¼ cup caster sugar
1 egg yolk
½ cup canned unsweetened chestnut purée or whole chestnuts, drained and puréed
1 teaspoon vanilla essence
1 cup plain flour, sifted
¼ teaspoon cinnamon
caster sugar for coating
90 g dark chocolate, melted

1 Preheat oven to 180°C and grease baking trays.

2 Cream butter and sugar until light and fluffy. Beat in egg yolk, then chestnut purée and vanilla, and mix well. Sift together flour and cinnamon and beat

into creamed mixture.

3 To make each biscuit, roll on grease-proof paper with floured hands, two teaspoonfuls of dough into fingers about 6 cm long. Arrange on prepared trays and sprinkle lightly with caster sugar. Bake for 20 minutes until well browned. Cool completely.

4 Dip one end of each finger diagonally into melted, cooled chocolate. Cool for 5–10 minutes on a greaseproof paper-lined tray until set.

Carrot and Raisin Rounds

These fruity biscuits have a crispy crust but the centres are nice and chewy — and just look at the number you can make from one batch.

PREPARATION TIME: *15 minutes*
COOKING TIME: *15 minutes per batch*
MAKES 36

125 g butter
¾ cup raw sugar
1 egg
1 cup finely grated carrot
¼ cup finely chopped walnuts
½ cup finely chopped raisins
1 cup self-raising flour
¼ cup plain flour
1 teaspoon cinnamon
½ teaspoon nutmeg
¼ teaspoon ground cloves
¾ cup coarsely ground toasted muesli
¼–½ cup plain low-fat yoghurt

1 Preheat oven to 190°C and grease oven trays.

2 Cream butter, add sugar and egg and beat well. Stir in carrot, walnuts, raisins and three-quarters of sifted dry ingredients. Add muesli, remaining sifted dry ingredients and sufficient yoghurt to make a firm dough.

3 Place slightly heaped teaspoonfuls of mixture at intervals on prepared trays, press down tops with a fork and bake 12–15 minutes or until golden brown.

4 Cool on trays 10 minutes before removing to a cake rack to cool completely. May be iced with a lemon glacé icing if desired.

To quickly firm up biscuit doughs for easier handling, wrap dough in plastic wrap and place in freezer for one-third of the time you would normally refrigerate it.

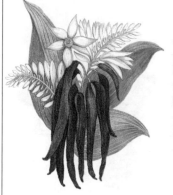

Step 1 Stir sifted flour and baking powder gradually into creamed mixture.

Step 2 Using a piping bag fitted with a star tube, pipe out mixture to form 4 cm lengths on trays.

Step 3 Join fingers together with coffee cream.

Coffee Fingers

For quick filling between these biscuits, replace coffee cream with a chocolate hazelnut spread.

PREPARATION TIME: *45 minutes*
COOKING TIME: *7 minutes per batch*
MAKES ABOUT 20

250 g butter
½ cup icing sugar, sifted
½ teaspoon vanilla essence
2 cups plain flour, sifted
¼ teaspoon baking powder
FILLING
45 g butter
1 teaspoon instant coffee powder dissolved in 1½ teaspoons hot water
1 cup icing sugar, sifted

1 Preheat oven to 190°C and grease oven trays.

2 Cream butter, icing sugar and vanilla until light and fluffy. Sift together flour and baking powder, and gradually stir into creamed mixture until ingredients are well mixed.

3 Place dough in a pastry bag fitted with a large star tube. Press out to form 4 cm lengths on prepared trays. If dough does not press smoothly, stir in 2 teaspoons softened butter. Bake for 5–7 minutes until edges start to brown. Cool for five minutes on trays before turning out onto wire racks to cool further.

4 To prepare filling: cream butter, add dissolved coffee and gradually beat in icing sugar. Join two fingers together with filling. Repeat with remaining biscuits.

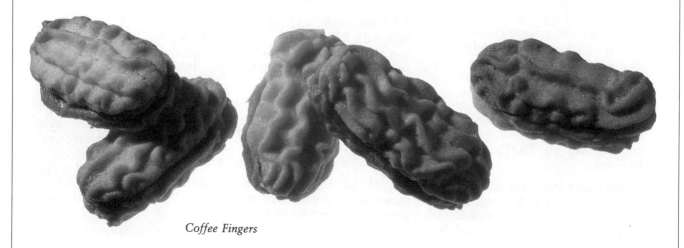

Coffee Fingers

Shortbread Fancies

To keep biscuits fresh, store unfilled shortbread in an airtight container and join biscuits with butter cream close to serving time.

PREPARATION TIME: *40 minutes*
COOKING TIME: *25 minutes per batch*
MAKES ABOUT 36

250 g butter, softened
1 teaspoon vanilla
¾ cup icing sugar, sifted
2 cups plain flour
LEMON ICING
40 g butter, softened
1¼ cups icing sugar, sifted
1–2 teaspoons lemon juice
finely grated rind of ½ lemon
extra icing sugar for dusting

1 Preheat oven to 150°C and grease oven trays.

2 Cream butter, vanilla and icing sugar until light and fluffy. Add sifted flour and combine to form a stiff dough.

3 Roll pieces of dough into balls about the size of large marbles. Arrange on prepared trays. Flatten balls with a fork. Bake for 20–25 minutes, or until firm and pale golden. Stand on tray five minutes before carefully lifting to a wire rack to cool.

4 To prepare icing: beat together butter, icing sugar, lemon juice and lemon rind until pale and fluffy. Join two biscuits together and dust with sifted icing sugar. Repeat until biscuits are complete.

Shortbread Nut Cookies

For an almond flavour, use almond essence to replace the vanilla and top with blanched almonds.

PREPARATION TIME: *25 minutes plus 30 minutes chilling time*
COOKING TIME: *12 minutes per batch*
MAKES ABOUT 36

125 g butter
⅓ cup caster sugar
1 teaspoon vanilla essence
1 egg yolk
1 cup plain flour, sifted
½ cup self-raising flour, sifted
60 g roasted hazelnuts or blanched almonds

1 Cream butter and sugar together until light and fluffy. Beat in vanilla and egg yolk and mix well. Add sifted flours and combine to form a stiff dough.

2 Roll into a sausage shape, wrap in greaseproof paper and refrigerate for 30 minutes.

3 Preheat oven to 180°C and grease oven trays.

4 Slice dough into 3 mm rounds. Arrange on prepared trays. Press a nut on top of each round. Bake for 12 minutes.

5 Cool on tray for a few minutes. Remove to a wire rack to cool completely. Store in an airtight container.

Shortbread is a Scottish speciality enjoyed year round but especially baked for New Year celebrations. The secret to crisp yet tender shortbread is in the kneading. Gently knead the dough on a lightly floured surface for 10 to 15 minutes and the shortbread will become very smooth and buttery.

Shortbread Fancies

Shortbread Nut Cookies

Slices

Sweet and Sensational

MORE BODY THAN BISCUITS and more petite than cakes, slices are fabulous for late-night suppers with coffee, or by day for school and office lunches. Whether baked or unbaked, appetising slices keep well and are handy to have in your pantry when surprise visitors drop in.

Try our recipes for Chocolate Temptation Slice, Fantasy Slice or the fruity Apricot Slice.

Apricot Slice, Date Slice Delight and Fruity Pumpkin Bars (page 84) 81

Buttermilk can substitute for milk in recipes, giving a very moist result. You will need the addition of a binding agent, for example an egg or flour in the recipe to prevent curdling.

Pointers for perfection

Slices are most easily cooked in a shallow oblong or slab tin about 18 x 28 cm. The tin should be well greased but there is usually no need to line the base with paper, as the slice is left in the tin until cool. Cut into even slices and remove with a palette knife or spatula when quite cold.

The best way to cut a slice is to cut it in half, then cut each half in half lengthways; then cut the slice in half across the width and finally cut each half into thirds.

Most cake recipes can be iced while still in the tin. A 'slice' of cake is also easier to eat than a 'wedge', and is ideal for picnics, for example.

The section includes several recipes which do not require baking. Most of these are rich with chocolate, making them ideal to serve with coffee.

Fantasy Slice

You can substitute white chocolate for dark to give a coffee coloured slice with fruits and nuts deliciously visible. You can use any stale or unpopular biscuits in the biscuit barrel to replace the shortbread in this recipe.

PREPARATION TIME: *20 minutes*
COOKING TIME: *5 minutes*
MAKES ABOUT 20

375 g shortbread biscuits, finely crushed
60 g walnuts, chopped
200 g desiccated coconut
100 g chocolate, finely grated
185 g butter
2 tablespoons honey
1 cup chopped glacé fruit
3 tablespoons Tia Maria
ICING
40 g butter
1 cup icing sugar
60 g chocolate, melted
1 tablespoon instant coffee dissolved in
3 tablespoons hot water

1 Lightly brush an 18 x 28 cm shallow tin with oil.

2 In a bowl mix biscuits, nuts, coconut and chocolate. In a pan, heat butter and honey, stirring to combine. Pour over biscuit mix and combine with fruit and liqueur. Press mixture firmly into prepared tin and set aside.

3 To prepare icing: cream butter and icing sugar. Stir in melted chocolate and coffee, and combine well. Spread smoothly over slice and chill. Slice into pieces to serve.

Toasted Almond Slices

This topping sets firmly on cooling. To make slicing easier, cut into slices while still slightly warm. Cool completely before removing from tin.

PREPARATION TIME: *35 minutes*
COOKING TIME: *40 minutes*
MAKES ABOUT 16

BASE
125 g butter, softened
½ cup icing sugar
1 cup plain flour, sifted
ALMOND TOPPING
½ cup brown sugar
40 g butter
1 tablespoon water
1 tablespoon lemon juice
¾ cup flaked almonds
¾ teaspoon vanilla essence

1 Preheat oven to 180°C and line a 20 cm square cake tin with greaseproof paper.

2 To prepare base: cream butter and icing sugar until fluffy using medium speed of an electric mixer. Add flour and mix well.

3 Press mixture into prepared tin and bake for 15 minutes.

4 In a pan, combine sugar, butter, water and lemon juice. Heat to boiling, stirring constantly to dissolve sugar completely. Remove from heat. Stir in almonds and vanilla.

5 Spread topping carefully over partially baked crust. Continue baking 15–20 minutes until topping is set and golden. Cool on a wire rack. Cut into slices to serve and remove paper.

Anna's Continental Apple Cake

This moist apple cake is best eaten within two days of baking. It can also be served as a dessert with whipped cream.

PREPARATION TIME: *45 minutes*
COOKING TIME: *40 minutes*
MAKES ABOUT 48

125 g butter
½ cup sugar
2 eggs
1 x 300 ml carton sour cream
1 teaspoon bicarbonate of soda
2 cups self-raising flour, sifted
2 green cooking apples, peeled, cored and sliced
TOPPING
½ cup chopped walnuts
2 tablespoons sugar
1 teaspoon cinnamon

1 Preheat oven to 180°C. Grease and line a 26 x 30 cm baking tin.

2 To prepare base: cream butter and sugar until light and fluffy. Beat in eggs one at a time, mixing well after each addition. Beat in sour cream and soda. Add flour, folding lightly into mixture.

3 Pour mixture into prepared tin. Arrange apples on top. Combine topping ingredients and sprinkle over apples.

4 Bake for 35–40 minutes. Cool in tin. Cut into squares to serve, remove paper and store in an airtight container.

Anna's Continental Apple Cake

Muesli Slice

Muesli Slice

Add ¼ cup of chocolate chips to this recipe and ice with a lemon glacé icing for variation.

PREPARATION TIME: *10 minutes*
COOKING TIME: *25 minutes*
MAKES ABOUT 20

2 cups rolled oats
½ cup brown sugar
½ cup unsalted peanuts
½ cup desiccated coconut
125 g butter, melted

1 Preheat oven to 180°C. Lightly brush an 18 x 28 cm shallow tin with oil.

2 Combine all ingredients in a bowl and mix well. Turn mixture into prepared tin.

3 Bake for 20–25 minutes until golden. Cut into squares to serve.

Apricot Slice

This fruity slice is filled with health and fibre. A great slice for the school lunch box.

PREPARATION TIME: *25 minutes*
COOKING TIME: *35 minutes*
MAKES ABOUT 24

½ cup self-raising flour, sifted
½ cup untoasted muesli
¼ cup rolled oats
¼ cup desiccated coconut
½ cup brown sugar
½ cup chopped dried apricots
¼ cup sultanas
180 g butter
2 tablespoons honey or golden syrup
2 eggs, lightly beaten

1 Preheat oven to 180°C and grease an 18 x 28 cm shallow tin.

2 Combine flour, muesli, oats, coconut, sugar and fruit in a bowl. Melt butter and honey together in a small pan. Pour over dry ingredients and mix well.

3 Stir in eggs. Blend in well. Press mixture into prepared tin and bake for 30 minutes.

4 Cool in tin. Cut when cold and store in an airtight container.

Date Slice Delight

Date slices are always popular. This variation is delightful. It will store well in an airtight container for up to four days.

PREPARATION TIME: *45 minutes*
COOKING TIME: *50 minutes*
MAKES ABOUT 48

250 g pitted dates
1½ cups orange juice
2½ cups plain flour
1¼ cups brown sugar
375 g butter, cut in pieces
1 cup desiccated coconut
1 cup chopped pecans or walnuts
1½ cups rolled oats

1 Preheat oven to 180°C and grease a 26 x 30 cm baking tin.

2 Simmer dates in orange juice, stirring

occasionally until thickened. Remove from heat.

3 Combine flour and sugar. Rub in butter until crumbly. Stir in coconut, pecans and oats, and mix well.

4 Press half the mixture into prepared tin, patting flat. Spread with date mixture to 1 cm from edges. Top with remaining oat mixture and press flat.

5 Bake for 45–50 minutes until firm and golden. Cool in tin before cutting.

Fruity Pumpkin Bars

For a delicious topping, mix together 300 ml sour cream and 1 cup brown sugar. Pour over slice 10 minutes before cooking time is complete. Topping will set as slice cools. Cool in tin before cutting.

PREPARATION TIME: *30 minutes*
COOKING TIME: *35 minutes*
MAKES 24

1½ cups wholemeal self-raising flour
⅓ cup raw sugar
½ cup raisins or sultanas
½ cup chopped, dried peaches, apricots or apples
½ teaspoon nutmeg
1 egg
125 g butter, melted
¼ cup buttermilk or soured milk
2 tablespoons golden syrup
1 cup drained, mashed, cooked pumpkin

1 Preheat oven to 190°C and grease an 18 x 28 cm shallow tin.

2 In a large bowl, stir together flour, sugar, dried fruits and nutmeg. Add remaining ingredients and beat with a wooden spoon until well blended.

3 Pour into prepared tin and bake for 30–35 minutes until top springs back when gently pressed. Cool and cut into slices to serve.

Freeze any leftover boiled or steamed pumpkin for use in cakes and scones. Cooked potato may also be used. Shredded zucchini and carrot also give moist results.

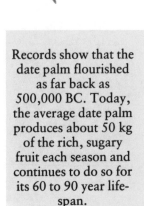

Records show that the date palm flourished as far back as 500,000 BC. Today, the average date palm produces about 50 kg of the rich, sugary fruit each season and continues to do so for its 60 to 90 year life-span.

Fantasy Slice, Toasted Almond Slice, Chocolate Flake Slice (page 88)

Coconut Meringue Slice

For extra flavour, spread ½ cup warm jam or lemon cheese over base before topping with meringue.

PREPARATION TIME: *40 minutes*
COOKING TIME: *30 minutes*
MAKES ABOUT 24

125 g butter
1 cup caster sugar
2 eggs, separated
1 cup self-raising flour, sifted
1 cup desiccated coconut

1 Preheat oven to 180°C and grease an 18 x 28 cm shallow tin.

2 Cream butter and ½ cup sugar until light and fluffy. Beat in egg yolks and mix well.

3 Mix in flour. Spread over base of prepared tin using lightly floured fingertips.

4 Beat egg whites until stiff peaks form. Gradually add remaining sugar. Beat until thick and glossy. Fold in coconut using a metal spoon.

5 Spread over base. Bake for 25–30 minutes or until cooked when tested with a skewer. Cool before cutting into squares to serve.

Step 1 *Cream butter and sugar, beat in egg yolks. Mix well.*

Step 2 *Spread over base of tin using lightly floured fingertips.*

Step 3 *Fold coconut into beaten egg white mixture using a metal spoon.*

Step 4 *Spread base with jam if desired. Top with coconut meringue.*

Coconut Meringue Slice

Chocolate Slice

Chocolate Slice

To cut Chocolate Slice easily, use a sharp knife that has been dipped in hot water.

PREPARATION TIME: *35 minutes*
COOKING TIME: *5 minutes*
MAKES ABOUT 36

BASE
125 g butter
½ cup caster sugar
3 tablespoons cocoa
1 egg, beaten
1 teaspoon vanilla essence
2 cups crushed wheatmeal biscuits
¾ cup desiccated coconut
½ cup chopped walnuts
CUSTARD FILLING
60 g butter
1¾ cups icing sugar
2 tablespoons custard powder
2 tablespoons hot water
CHOCOLATE TOPPING

60 g unsalted butter
125 g cooking chocolate

1 Grease an 18 x 28 cm shallow tin.

2 To prepare base: combine butter, sugar and cocoa in a pan. Stir over low heat until melted and well blended. Stir in egg and vanilla. Cook, stirring, 1 minute. Remove from heat.

3 Combine biscuit crumbs, coconut and walnuts in a large bowl. Pour in butter mixture and mix well. Press into prepared tin and refrigerate until set.

4 To prepare filling: cream butter, sift icing sugar and custard powder together. Add to butter alternately with hot water. Beat until fluffy. Spread over base and refrigerate until set.

5 To prepare topping: melt butter in a pan over low heat. Add chocolate. Stir to combine while melting. Pour over custard topping. Refrigerate until set. Cut into fingers to serve. Keep refrigerated.

Where did the coconut originate? No one seems to know, but it is recorded that the origin of the word 'coconut' comes from the sixteenth-century explorers, who noticed that the three scars on the base of the coconut shell resembled a monkey's face. So they called the nut 'coco', which was the Spanish slang word for monkey face.

Magic Biscuit Bars

This recipe has the title of 'Magic' Biscuit Bars because of its no-bowl, no-mess method. The biscuit comes together in the baking.

PREPARATION TIME: *20 minutes*
COOKING TIME: *30 minutes*
MAKES ABOUT 24

125 g butter, melted
1½ cups plain biscuit crumbs
1 cup chopped pecans or walnuts
1 x 100 g packet chocolate bits
1¼ cups desiccated coconut
1 x 400 ml can sweetened condensed milk

1 Preheat oven to 180°C. Line an 18 x 28 cm shallow tin with greaseproof paper.

2 Pour melted butter into prepared tin. Sprinkle biscuit crumbs evenly over butter and press lightly to form a crust.

3 Over crumbs, sprinkle nuts, chocolate bits and coconut. Pour milk evenly over all.

4 Bake for 25–30 minutes until lightly browned and set. Cool 15 minutes in tin on a wire rack. Cut into slices, remove paper and cool before serving.

To crush biscuits, place in a strong plastic bag and close top. Break biscuits up with the side of a rolling pin. Alternatively, use a food processor.

Magic Biscuit Bars

Chocolate Flake Slice

Crush muesli in a strong paper or plastic bag by gently hitting with a rolling pin. For a crunchy topping, sprinkle slice with a little extra toasted muesli. The texture contrast of a crunchy biscuit base and a smooth moist chocolate icing makes these slices most appealing. Top with chopped nuts if desired.

PREPARATION TIME: *35 minutes*
COOKING TIME: *20 minutes*
MAKES ABOUT 14

1 cup plain flour
1 teaspoon baking powder
2 tablespoons cocoa powder
¼ cup sugar
2 cups lightly crushed toasted muesli
1 egg, beaten
125 g butter, melted and cooled
CHOCOLATE ICING
3 tablespoons cocoa powder
1½ cups icing sugar, sifted
2 tablespoons hot milk
2 teaspoons butter
1 teaspoon vanilla essence

1 Preheat oven to 180°C and grease an 18 cm square sandwich cake tin.

2 Sift flour, baking powder and cocoa three times into a bowl. Add sugar, muesli, egg and butter, and combine well.

3 Press firmly into prepared tin and bake 15–20 minutes or until firm to the touch. Allow to cool in tin.

4 To prepare icing: sift cocoa and icing sugar into a bowl. Stir butter into hot milk until butter melts. Add sufficient milk mixture to icing sugar to form a spreading consistency. Stir in vanilla essence. Spread icing over slice and when set, cut into slices to serve.

Chocolate Flake Slice

Chocolate Temptation Slice

Substitute 250 g stale sponge or cake crumbs for biscuit crumbs. A splash of rum added to the chocolate mixture makes this slice ideal as a treat served with coffee.

PREPARATION TIME: *15 minutes*
COOKING TIME: *5 minutes*
MAKES ABOUT 12

125 g dark chocolate, chopped
125 g unsalted butter, cut into small pieces
2 tablespoons thickened cream
1 tablespoon golden syrup
125 g plain sweet biscuits, coarsely broken (not too crushed)
½ cup toasted flaked almonds
¼ cup raisins, chopped
2 tablespoons chopped glacé cherries

1 Lightly brush an 18 cm round sandwich tin with oil.

2 In a large bowl over barely simmering water, melt chocolate. Add butter pieces, cream and golden syrup. Stir until smooth. Cool slightly. Quickly mix in biscuits, almonds, raisins and cherries.

3 Turn mixture into prepared tin. Smooth the surface. Chill until set then slice into small portions as needed. Keep refrigerated.

Chocolate Honey Slices

Flavour chocolate topping with coffee flavoured liqueur and use hazelnuts in place of walnuts for a tempting variation of this recipe.

PREPARATION TIME: *30 minutes*
COOKING TIME: *35 minutes*
MAKES ABOUT 24

⅔ cup honey
250 g butter, melted and cooled
1 teaspoon vanilla essence
¼ teaspoon cinnamon
2 eggs, beaten
1½ cups self-raising flour
1¼ cups finely ground toasted muesli
CHOCOLATE TOPPING
185 g semi-sweet chocolate, chopped
½ cup icing sugar, sifted
3 tablespoons evaporated milk
30 g butter
½ cup chopped walnuts or almonds

1 Preheat oven to 180°C and grease an 18 x 28 cm shallow tin.

2 Combine honey, butter, vanilla, cinnamon and eggs in a bowl. Stir in flour and muesli, beating well to mix. Pour batter evenly into prepared tin and bake 25–30 minutes or until golden brown and firm to touch. Remove from the oven.

3 To prepare topping: place chocolate, icing sugar, milk and butter in the top half of a double saucepan. Stir over hot water until smooth. Spread over hot slice. Sprinkle with walnuts and cool in pan. Cut into slices to serve.

Liqueurs have a spirit base (usually brandy) that is blended with sugar syrup and flavoured with coffee beans, citrus oils, herbs and spices. Liqueurs have a natural affinity with desserts, cakes and after-dinner coffee.

Chocolate Temptation Slice

Chocolate Honey Slice

Fête Fare

All the Fun of the Fair

ROLL UP, ROLL UP for all the fun of the fair! Every kind of cake, biscuit and slice imaginable. Fêtes are a wonderful opportunity to roll up your sleeves and bake for a worthy cause.

What could be more popular than delicious homebaked treats, beautifully wrapped and presented?

As well as a selection of everyone's favourite biscuits, we've included classic scone and muffin recipes for the refreshments stall and lots of yummy nibbles and munchies for the children. For fête bakers who always have a budget to keep to, our recipes are inexpensive and quick to prepare. Most freeze well and can be prepared well in advance of the big day.

The river is forbidden,
The brook has run quite dry ;
There might be fishes hidden
Here in the tub—let's try !

Lamingtons are Australian cakes, supposedly named after Baron Lamington, Governor of Queensland from 1895 to 1901. The most popular lamington is a basic butter cake cut into squares, dipped in chocolate icing and coated with desiccated coconut.

Pointers for perfection

To a non-cook, nothing is as popular as home-baked cakes or biscuits — that's why there is always a rush to the cake stall at fêtes.

If you are the cook, select cakes or biscuits that are inexpensive and quick to prepare — it's always better to make two rather than one. It's also a good idea to choose recipes that freeze, so you can prepare them several weeks in advance.

Sponge cakes freeze well — just fill with jam and whipped cream on the day. It's always best to ice on the day (cream cheese frostings, however, freeze well).

Make sure your cake or biscuits will be easy to decorate, wrap and transport. You may need to take some of the makings, such as whipped cream, to the fête and arrive early, to finish the final assembly.

We've included some classic scone and muffin recipes to serve on a morning or afternoon tea stall, and delicious nibbles and crunchies for the children to snack on.

Lamingtons

These all-time favourites will be 'best sellers' on your stall.

PREPARATION TIME: *1½ hours*
COOKING TIME: *30 minutes*
MAKES 24

125 g butter
¾ cup caster sugar
2 eggs
½ teaspoon vanilla essence
2 cups self-raising flour, sifted
½ cup milk
250 g desiccated coconut
MOCK CREAM
2 tablespoons water
¼ cup sugar
60 g butter
few drops vanilla essence
CHOCOLATE ICING
500 g icing sugar
¼ cup cocoa
⅓ cup boiling water
1 teaspoon butter
few drops vanilla essence

1 Preheat oven to 180°C. Grease and line an 18 x 28 cm shallow tin.

2 Cream butter and sugar together until light and fluffy. Add eggs one at a time, beating well after each addition. Add vanilla. Fold in flour alternately with milk, beginning and ending with flour.

3 Pour into prepared tin. Bake 30 minutes or until cooked when tested. Cool on a wire rack. Store overnight. Slice cake in half horizontally.

4 To prepare cream: heat water and sugar in small pan, stirring until mixture boils. Remove from heat and cool. Cream butter in a small bowl using an electric beater. Pour cold syrup in a thin stream into butter. Beat well. Flavour with vanilla. Spread base of cake with mock cream. Place other layer on top. Chill until cream sets firm. Cut into 24 pieces.

5 To prepare icing: sift icing sugar and cocoa into bowl. Stir in remaining ingredients. Mix until smooth. Dip pieces into chocolate icing. Roll immediately in coconut. Stand on a wire rack until set. Store in an airtight container until required.

Turkish Delight

This quick method results in a tasty confection more like French jellies than the true Turkish Delight, but you're sure to find it just as delightful!

PREPARATION TIME: *45 minutes*
COOKING TIME: *20 minutes*
MAKES ABOUT 36

2 tablespoons plain gelatine
1 cup water
2 cups caster sugar
¼ cup unblanched almonds, toasted and coarsely chopped (optional)
1–1½ teaspoons rosewater or orange-flower water
few drops red or yellow food colour
⅓ cup icing sugar, sifted
1 tablespoon cornflour

Almond Toast,
Turkish Delight,
Chocolate Peanut Bites
and Apricot Nibbles

1 Lightly brush a 20 cm square tin with oil.

2 Soften gelatine in ½ cup water. Set aside. In a pan, combine sugar and remaining water.

3 Heat slowly until boiling, stirring to dissolve sugar. Boil rapidly to 110°C on a sugar thermometer, or until a teaspoonful of the syrup forms a gel when dropped into cold water.

4 Stir in gelatine mixture until dissolved. Remove from heat. Stir in almonds (if using), flavouring and colour.

5 Pour mixture into a prepared tin and cool completely. Cut into 2.5 cm squares with a sharp, oiled knife.

6 Combine icing sugar and cornflour. Toss squares in mixture to coat. Place in airtight container, sprinkling between layers with any remaining sugar mixture. Keep cool.

Almond Toast

Slice partially cooked loaf and freeze. Bake as many slices as required at any time straight from freezer. A combination of macadamia nuts, pecans, walnuts and pistachios makes a delicious alternative to almonds. Beautiful biscuits to serve with tea, after dinner or as an accompaniment to soft desserts, such as mousse.

PREPARATION TIME: *1 hour*
COOKING TIME: *45 minutes*
MAKES ABOUT 36

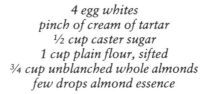

4 egg whites
pinch of cream of tartar
½ cup caster sugar
1 cup plain flour, sifted
¾ cup unblanched whole almonds
few drops almond essence

1 Preheat oven to 200°C and grease a small loaf tin.

2 Beat egg whites with cream of tartar until stiff peaks form. Gradually add sugar, beating constantly until stiff. Lightly fold in flour, almonds and essence.

3 Spoon mixture into prepared tin and bake 30–35 minutes. Cool for five minutes, then turn out onto a wire rack to cool completely.

4 Cut loaf into wafer-thin slices with a sharp, thin-bladed knife. Place on an ungreased baking tray. Reduce oven temperature to 150°C and bake again for 10–12 minutes. Cool and store in an airtight container.

Toffee Apples

Amaranth powder is the red colouring once used by pharmacists in the preparation of medications. Your local chemist may have a jar, so stock up (a little goes a long way) for professional-looking toffee apples. Otherwise, use liquid food colour, cochineal, or red powdered Chinese food colouring available from Asian provision stores.

PREPARATION TIME: *45 minutes*
COOKING TIME: *30 minutes*
MAKES 20

20 small red apples
4 cups sugar
1 cup water
½ teaspoon cream of tartar
¼ teaspoon amaranth powder or
2–3 teaspoons liquid food colour

1 Wipe apples thoroughly with a clean, dry towel. Push a stick or skewer into stem of each.

2 In a large heavy covered pan, heat sugar and water slowly until boiling and sugar dissolves.

3 Add cream of tartar and amaranth powder. Boil, uncovered, to 130°C on a sugar thermometer, or until a teaspoonful of the syrup cracks when drizzled into cold water.

4 Remove from heat. Twist about half the apples, one at a time, into syrup to coat. Drain and place on greased baking tray.

5 Heat remaining syrup again until boiling. Remove from heat and coat remaining apples. Cool until set. Wrap in cellophane and tie with ribbon, if desired.

Date and Pecan Loaf

This cake freezes well. When cold, wrap and freeze. Delicious topped with coffee icing or cream cheese frosting.

PREPARATION TIME: *25 minutes*
COOKING TIME: *50 minutes*
MAKES 1 CAKE

90 g butter, chopped
1 cup brown sugar
1 cup chopped dates

½ cup chopped pecans
1 cup boiling water
1¾ cups self-raising flour, sifted
½ teaspoon cinnamon
½ teaspoon ground ginger

1 Preheat oven to 180°C. Grease and line a 23 x 13 cm loaf tin.

2 Combine butter, sugar, dates and pecans in a large bowl. Mix well. Add water. Stir until butter has melted. Fold in remaining ingredients.

3 Spoon mixture into prepared tin and bake for 45–50 minutes or until cooked when tested.

4 Cool on a wire rack. Store in an airtight container. Serve sliced and buttered.

Apricot Nibbles

Ensure mixture is cool enough to handle before rolling with hands into balls.

PREPARATION TIME: *45 minutes*
COOKING TIME: *5 minutes*
MAKES ABOUT 48

125 g butter
1 cup sugar
⅓ cup plain flour
2 eggs
1 cup chopped dried apricots
1 teaspoon vanilla essence
3 cups wheatflake cereal, coarsely crushed
1 cup chopped pecans or walnuts
¾ cup icing sugar

1 Melt butter in pan and stir in sugar, flour, eggs and apricots.

2 Cook, stirring constantly, over moderate heat until flour cooks through and mixture is very thick, about five minutes. Remove from heat and stir in vanilla. Cool for five minutes.

3 Combine cereal and nuts in a large bowl. Add apricot mixture and mix thoroughly. Roll into 2.5 cm balls.

4 Roll balls in icing sugar to coat. Store between sheets of greaseproof paper in an airtight container or place in paper patty cases to serve.

Flavoured sugars are easy to make and are delightful additions to cakes, biscuits and slices. For vanilla sugar, add four or more vanilla pods to a 500 g jar of caster sugar. Stand for a week. Store in a cool dark place. For cinnamon sugar, simply add three sticks of cinnamon to castor sugar. Try cloves, cinnamon or aniseed for a spicy sugar.

Banana Cake

Sprinkle icing with desiccated coconut before wrapping and freezing. This helps prevent the icing from sticking to the freezer wrap.

PREPARATION TIME: *50 minutes*
COOKING TIME: *40 minutes*
MAKES 1 CAKE

125 g butter
½ cup brown sugar, firmly packed
2 eggs
1 cup mashed bananas
½ cup sour cream
2 cups self-raising flour, sifted
LEMON ICING
1½ cups icing sugar, sifted
15 g soft butter
1 teaspoon shredded lemon rind
2 tablespoons lemon juice

1 Preheat oven to 180°C. Grease a 23 x 13 cm loaf tin, line with greaseproof paper and grease paper.

2 Cream butter and sugar together until light and fluffy. Add eggs one at a time, beating well after each addition. Stir in mashed bananas and sour cream. Fold in flour.

3 Pour into prepared tin and bake for 40 minutes or until cooked when tested. Cool on a wire rack.

4 To prepare icing: combine all ingredients. Beat thoroughly until smooth and creamy. Spread over cooled cake. If desired, wrap well when cold and freeze.

Remember not to overbeat butter in cake and biscuit making. You may find extra flour is required, causing a heavy textured result.

Date and Pecan Loaf and Banana Cake

*Chocolate Date Slice
and Sesame Crunch*

Chocolate Date Slices

*Ice this slice with chocolate glacé icing
and place a walnut half on each square to
serve.*

PREPARATION TIME: *30 minutes*
COOKING TIME: *40 minutes*
MAKES ABOUT 48

*250 g chopped pitted dates
⅔ cup packed brown sugar
125 g butter
½ cup water
1 cup dark chocolate bits
2 eggs
1¼ cups self-raising flour
½ cup each orange juice and milk
1 cup finely chopped walnuts*

1 Preheat oven to 180°C and grease a
30 x 25 cm Swiss roll tin.

2 In a pan, combine dates, sugar, butter
and water. Heat until boiling, stirring to
dissolve sugar. Reduce heat. Simmer, stirring for five minutes until dates are soft.

3 Remove from heat. Stir in chocolate
until melted. Set aside to cool.

4 Beat in eggs, one at a time. Stir in flour
alternately with orange juice and milk
until mixture is well blended. Fold in
chopped walnuts.

5 Spread evenly into prepared tin and
bake for about 30 minutes until a
toothpick inserted in the centre comes out
clean. Cool completely and cut into small
squares to serve.

Sesame Crunch

*This slice also tastes delicious dipped in
melted chocolate.
Do not store this slice in the refrigerator
as it will become soft and sticky.*

PREPARATION TIME: *30 minutes*
COOKING TIME: *10 minutes*
MAKES ABOUT 24

*2 cups sesame seeds
½ cup honey
½ cup brown sugar
½ teaspoon ground ginger
½ teaspoon cinnamon*

1 Line an 18 x 28 cm shallow tin with
lightly oiled greaseproof paper or baking
paper.

2 Stir sesame seeds in a small pan over
low heat until lightly toasted (do not
overbrown). Transfer to a bowl to cool.

3 In a small pan, combine remaining
ingredients. Cook over low heat, stirring
until sugar dissolves and mixture boils.

4 Boil for two minutes without stirring.
Fold in sesame seeds and pour at once
into prepared tin, spreading evenly. Cool
15–20 minutes.

5 Remove crunch from tin with its paper
attached. With a sharp knife, cut into
small fingers or squares. Cool completely,
then peel off paper. Wrap pieces individually or store between layers of plastic
wrap in an airtight container.

Neenish Tarts

Here's a modern approach to a really old-fashioned bakery favourite!

These are delicious made with a fresh cream filling. Beat 300 ml cream with 2 tablespoons caster sugar and 1 teaspoon rum. Spoon over jam and chill. Make sure cream is firm before icing.

If desired, at Step 5, omit chocolate and tint one portion of the icing with pink or yellow food colour.

Step 1 *Place pastry rounds in tins, piercing well to prevent puffing.*

PREPARATION TIME: *1 hour*
COOKING TIME: *10 minutes*
MAKES 12

1 sheet frozen, ready-rolled shortcrust
pastry, thawed
⅓ cup red jam
40 g butter, softened
½ cup icing sugar
2 teaspoons cream or milk
few drops rum or almond essence
ICING
1 cup icing sugar, sifted
1 teaspoon vanilla essence
a little hot water
60 g dark chocolate, melted and cooled

Step 2 *Place a teaspoon of jam into each baked tart.*

Rum is the distilled spirit of sugar cane. Light or white rum is best for cooking, though dark overproof rum is preferred for macerating dried fruits for rich dark fruit cakes.

1 Preheat oven to 220°C. For this recipe use ungreased patty tins.

2 Cut pastry into 12 circles to line patty tins. Place in tins, piercing well with a fork to prevent puffing. Bake for 10 minutes until crisp and golden. Remove from tins and cool.

3 Place a teaspoon of jam into each tart. Beat butter and icing sugar until fluffy. Beat in cream and rum until smooth and creamy. Spoon into tarts to cover jam.

Step 3 *Place a teaspoon of buttercream into each tart.*

4 To prepare icing: stir together sugar, vanilla and enough hot water to make a spreadable glaze. Divide in half. Stir cooled chocolate into one portion and thin slightly with hot water.

5 Spread icing over top of tarts, making each tart half white, half chocolate. Stand until icing sets.

Step 4 *Spread icing over top of tarts, making each tart half white, half chocolate.*

97

Coconut Carrot Muffins and Apple Cheese Scones

Coconut Carrot Muffins

You can use this recipe to make two large loaves in two greased and lined 23 x 13 cm loaf tins, baking at the same temperature for 1 hour.

PREPARATION TIME: *40 minutes*
COOKING TIME: *25 minutes*
MAKES 24

4 eggs
1 cup brown sugar
½ cup caster sugar
¾ cup vegetable oil
2 cups self-raising flour
2 teaspoons cinnamon
½ teaspoon nutmeg
¼ teaspoon mixed spice
2 cups shredded, peeled carrots
1 cup drained, canned crushed pineapple
½ cup desiccated coconut
CREAM CHEESE FILLING
1 x 250 g packet cream cheese,
softened
60 g butter, softened
2 teaspoons vanilla essence
3–3½ cups icing sugar, sifted

1 Preheat oven to 180°C. Grease and line with baking paper 24 large muffin tins or use paper cases.

2 In a large bowl, beat eggs until frothy. Gradually beat in sugars, then oil until blended. Sift together flour and spices. Fold into egg mixture with carrots, pineapple and coconut. Stir until only just combined.

3 Spoon into prepared muffin tins, filling two-thirds full. Bake for about 25 minutes until a skewer inserted in the centre comes out clean. Cool slightly in tins. Remove to wire racks and cool completely.

4 To prepare icing: beat together cream cheese and butter until creamy. Beat in vanilla. Gradually add icing sugar, beating until smooth. Spread over muffins.

Apple Cheese Scones

As a variation you can replace nuts with crunchy grain cereal; or add sultanas to scone mixture.

PREPARATION TIME: *35 minutes*
COOKING TIME: *20 minutes*
MAKES 18

1¾ cups self-raising flour
90 g shredded tasty cheese
30 g butter, chopped
1 small apple, peeled, cored and cut into
eighths
⅓–½ cup water
60 g butter, melted
⅓ cup sugar
⅓ cup chopped nuts
½ teaspoon cinnamon or nutmeg

1 Preheat oven to 190°C and grease a baking tray.

2 Combine flour, cheese and butter in a food processor container and process until mixture resembles breadcrumbs. Add apple with machine running and sufficient water to mix to a soft dough. Do not overprocess.

3 Turn dough onto a lightly floured board and divide into 18 equal pieces. Coat each piece with melted butter and toss in combined sugar, nuts and cinnamon.

4 Arrange scones on prepared tray and bake for 17–20 minutes or until nicely browned. Turn onto a wire rack and cover with a clean tea-towel while cooling.

Muffins are absurdly easy to make — simply follow the "Muffin Method". Add the combined liquid ingredients to combined dry ingredients with a few quick strokes. The mixture should in fact be still lumpy, the result light, fine-textured muffins.

Chocolate Peanut Bites

This recipe can be halved easily, if you prefer. Use a 20 or 23 cm square tin.

PREPARATION TIME: *30 minutes*
COOKING TIME: *nil*
MAKES ABOUT 20

3 cups icing sugar
¾ cup brown sugar
125 g butter, softened
2 cups peanut butter
1 cup unsalted peanuts (optional)
250 g dark chocolate
20 g extra butter

1 Beat together sugars and butter until blended — mixture will be crumbly. Mix in peanut butter and nuts, if using.

2 Press into an ungreased 30 x 25 cm tin, smoothing the surface.

3 Melt chocolate with the extra butter until smooth. Spread over peanut layer. Stand until set. Cut into 2.5 cm pieces.

Oatmeal Sultana Biscuits

Stir through chopped nuts such as walnuts, almonds, peanuts or cashews in place of half the fruit or chocolate bits.

PREPARATION TIME: *25 minutes*
COOKING TIME: *17 minutes per batch*
MAKES ABOUT 50

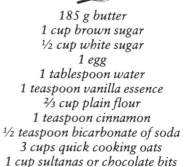

185 g butter
1 cup brown sugar
½ cup white sugar
1 egg
1 tablespoon water
1 teaspoon vanilla essence
⅔ cup plain flour
1 teaspoon cinnamon
½ teaspoon bicarbonate of soda
3 cups quick cooking oats
1 cup sultanas or chocolate bits

1 Preheat oven to 200°C and grease baking trays.

2 Beat together butter and sugars until fluffy. Beat in egg, then water and vanilla essence.

3 Sift together flour, cinnamon and soda three times. Stir in egg mixture, mixing well. Fold in oats and sultanas.

4 Drop level tablespoonfuls onto prepared trays, leaving room for spreading. Bake for 15–17 minutes until edges are browned, but centres still soft. Cool on racks. Store in an airtight container.

Chocolate Peanut Bites

Oatmeal Sultana Biscuits

Peanut Crunchy Bars

You can replace cornflakes with rice krispies or another similar breakfast cereal. Use a large metal spoon for mixing to avoid crushing cereal. This mixture can be spooned into patty paper cups to make individual servings.

PREPARATION TIME: *15 minutes*
COOKING TIME: *5 minutes*
MAKES 36

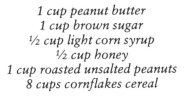

1 cup peanut butter
1 cup brown sugar
½ cup light corn syrup
½ cup honey
1 cup roasted unsalted peanuts
8 cups cornflakes cereal

1 In large pan, combine butter, sugar, syrup and honey. Stir over moderate heat until smooth and melted.

2 Remove from heat. Stir in peanuts, then quickly fold in cornflakes until coated (try not to crush them).

3 Pat mixture evenly into an oiled 33 x 25 cm shallow tin. Chill in freezer for 30 minutes before cutting into squares or spooning into paper cake cases. Store in airtight containers in refrigerator.

Peanut Crunchy Bars

Rocky Road Bars

Use kitchen scissors dipped in hot water to neatly cut marshmallows.

PREPARATION TIME: *30 minutes*
COOKING TIME: *50 minutes*
MAKES 48

185 g butter, softened
¾ cup sugar
2 eggs
1½ cups plain flour
4 tablespoons cocoa
¾ teaspoon bicarbonate of soda
1 cup chopped pecans or walnuts
¾ cup Smarties
⅔ cup cut-up marshmallows

1 Preheat oven to 180°C and grease an 18 x 28 cm shallow tin.

2 Beat together butter and sugar until light and creamy. Beat in eggs, one at a time, until blended.

3 Stir together flour, cocoa and soda. Gradually stir into creamed mixture until just combined (do not overmix). Fold in ½ cup nuts.

4 Spread mixture into prepared tin and bake for 45 minutes or until firm to touch. Sprinkle top with Smarties, marshmallows and remaining nuts; press lightly into cake.

5 Return to oven for 5 minutes until marshmallows are soft. Cover completely with foil. Cool on a wire rack. Cut into slices to serve.

Rocky Road Bars

Peanuts, which are also known as groundnuts, are actually members of the legume family. The nuts themselves are popular the world over, not only as a snack, but as a valuable contribution to vegetarian diets. Peanut oil is the cooking medium throughout Asia.

PACKAGING FOR FÊTE FOOD

PRICING IS TRICKY, but don't sell items too cheaply. It is a good idea to work out how much each recipe costs you to produce by itemising ingredients. If it's a cake, add about half as much again to the amount to reach a suitable price. For sweets, wrap them decoratively, divide the number of sweets in each package into the total of ingredients cost, add cost of packaging materials and you have the cost price per package. You can add on half as much again, to each package, if you are fundraising.

Have a good supply of paper bags and cake boxes to pack things into.

Try to keep the price down on some of the small items (e.g. chocolate crackles, patty cakes, etc) for children to buy.

For packaging use clear or coloured cellophane, tissue paper, paper plates wrapped in cellophane, small plastic boxes (available from speciality kitchen and chocolate shops), paper or cane baskets and doilies tied with ribbon. For popcorn, sell in disposable cups decorated with ribbon or make cardboard cones.

About half an hour before the fête is due to close, announce a cut in prices and watch your stall sell out — if it hasn't already!

GUIDE TO FREEZING

Large Cakes

Preparation
Bake in usual way, cool. Cakes are best frozen unfilled and undecorated. Uniced cakes are easier to pack. Glacé icing tends to weep and crack on thawing.

Freeze butter cream icing separately for up to 2 months and beat well after thawing.

Freezing
Open freeze all cakes to preserve shape. For this method place cake on a tray without covering. When frozen, wrap in plastic film and good quality aluminium foil, excluding as much air as possible. Store in an additional rigid container for added protection.

Storage time
3 months.

Thawing
Loosen wrapping and stand at room temperature for 1 to 3 hours according to size.

Slices, Muffins and Small Cakes

Preparation
Bake in the usual way, cool. Ice only if necessary.

Freezing
Careful freezing is required for small cakes. It is best to open freeze. Wrap separately when frozen and pack directly into a rigid container. Label and date.

Storage time
3 months.

Thawing
Cakes and slices should be thawed at room temperature in their wrapping, small iced cakes need to have wrapping loosened to prevent lifting the icing. Muffins may be wrapped in foil and heated in a moderate oven for 10 to 12 minutes.

Sponge Cakes

Preparation
Sponge cakes have very little fat and freeze well. Freeze sponges without jam or cream fillings.

Sponge rolls are best rolled in cornflour, not sugar, for freezing, to prevent cracking.

Freezing
Open freeze. Wrap as for large cakes. Label and date.

Storage time
3 months.

Thawing
As for large cakes.

Fruit Cakes

Preparation
Rich, dark fruit cakes mature and improve with keeping and there is really no need to freeze these cakes. Fruit cakes with low proportions of butter and those made by the 'rubbing' or 'melt and mix' methods can be successfully frozen. Individual slices or pieces of fruit cake may also be frozen.

Freezing
As for large cakes. Label and date.

Storage time
Boiled fruit cake — up to 6 months.

Thawing
As for large cakes. Fruit cake may take up to 3 to 4 hours to thaw.

Biscuits

Preparation
Biscuits are best frozen in their unbaked state.

Freezing
There are two methods of freezing biscuits. The dough may be made up into a roll and stored wrapped in foil. To use, cut off number of biscuits required and bake. Biscuits may also be shaped or cut out, open frozen on baking sheets, and then packed in rigid containers. Label and date.

Storage time
3 months.

Thawing
Biscuits should be baked from the frozen state. Place on baking tray, allowing a few extra minutes cooking time.

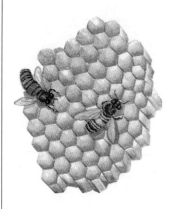

CONVERSION CHART

WEIGHTS AND MEASURES

Australian and American cooks use standard measuring cups for liquids and many solids, including flour, sugar, cocoa powder and prepared vegetables and fruits, whereas British cooks favour measuring jugs calibrated in millilitres and fluid ounces and scales calibrated in both metric and Imperial measures. The chart that follows gives equivalent metric, Imperial and standard cup measures. Please note that an American pint is equivalent to 16 fl oz whereas a British pint is 20 fl oz.

LIQUID MEASURES

Metric	Imperial	Standard Cup Measure
30 mL	1 fl oz	
60 mL	2 fl oz	¼ cup
75 mL	2½ fl oz	
80 mL	2¾ fl oz	⅓ cup
90 mL	3 fl oz	
125 mL	4 fl oz	½ cup
155 mL	5 fl oz	
170 mL	5½ fl oz	⅔ cup
185 mL	6 fl oz	¾ cup
220 mL	7 fl oz	
250 mL	8 fl oz	1 cup (½ US pint)
280 mL	9 fl oz	
315 mL	10 fl oz (½ pint)	1¼ cups
350 mL	11 fl oz	1⅓ cups
375 mL	12 fl oz	1½ cups
410 mL	13 fl oz	1⅔ cups
440 mL	14 fl oz	1 ¾ cups
470 mL	15 fl oz	
500 mL	16 fl oz	2 cups (1 US pint)
600 mL	20 fl oz (1 pint)	2½ cups
750 mL	1 pint 5 fl oz	3 cups
1 litre	1 pint 12 fl oz	4 cups
1.5 litres	2 pints 8 fl oz	6 cups

DRY MEASURES

Metric	Imperial
15 g	½ oz
30 g	1 oz
45 g	1½ oz
60 g	2 oz
90 g	3 oz
125 g	4 oz
155 g	5 oz
185 g	6 oz
220 g	7 oz
250 g	8 oz
280 g	9 oz
315 g	10 oz
350 g	11 oz
375 g	12 oz
410 g	13 oz
440 g	14 oz
470 g	15 oz
500 g	16 oz (1 lb)
750 g	1 lb 8 oz (1½ lb)
1 kg	2¼ lb
1.5 kg	3¼ lb
2 kg	4½ lb
2.5 kg	5½ lb

STANDARD CUP MEASURES

It is not possible to give a single standard cup measure for all dry ingredients as they all weigh different amounts; a cup of breadcrumbs, for instance, weighs 60 g/2 oz, whereas a cup of sugar weighs 250 g/8 oz. Some of the more common ingredients traditionally measured by cup in America and/or Australia are listed below:

Cup Measures	Metric/Imperial
1 cup butter or margarine (2 US sticks)	250 g/8 oz
1 cup grated hard cheese	125 g/4 oz
1 cup cream cheese/full fat soft cheese	250 g/8 oz
1 cup crumbled blue vein cheese	125–155 g/4–5 oz
1 cup plain/all-purpose flour	125 g/4 oz
1 cup wholemeal/wholewheat flour	140 g/4½ oz
1 cup crystalline/granulated sugar	250 g/8 oz
1 cup caster/superfine sugar	250 g/8 oz
1 cup icing/confectioners' sugar	155 g/5 oz
1 cup packed brown sugar	185 g/6 oz
1 cup chopped nuts	125 g/4 oz
1 cup soft/fresh breadcrumbs	60 g/2 oz
1 cup dry breadcrumbs	125 g/4 oz
1 cup raw rice	220 g/7 oz
1 cup cooked rice	125 g/4 oz
1 cup desiccated coconut	90 g/3 oz
1 cup cornflakes	25 g/1 oz
1 cup dried fruit (types vary)	155–185 g/5-6 oz
1 cup cooked mashed pumpkin	350 g/11 oz
1 cup pasta shapes	125 g/4 oz
1 cup chopped tomatoes	185 g/6 oz
1 cup chopped onion	125 g/4 oz
1 cup chopped capsicum/sweet pepper	125 g/4 oz
1 cup sliced mushrooms	125 g/4 oz
1 cup shelled peas	170 g/5½ oz
1 cup diced raw potato	185 g/6 oz
1 cup mashed potato	250 g/8 oz
1 cup diced apple	125 g/4 oz
1 cup apple purée (applesauce)	250 g/8 oz
1 cup black or redcurrants or blueberries	125 g/4 oz
1 cup raspberries or small strawberries	155 g/5 oz
1 cup honey, syrup or jam	350–375 g/11–12 oz
1 cup minced/ground beef or pork	250 g/8 oz

STANDARD SPOON MEASURES

When measuring by teaspoon (tsp) or tablespoon (tbsp), always use standard metric measuring spoons. While these are the same for Britain and the US (5 mL and 15 mL respectively), please note that the Australian standard tablespoon holds 20 mL and is therefore equivalent to 4 standard teaspoons. As recipes for this book were tested in Australia, British and American readers will need to adjust tablespoon quantities.

Australia	UK	US
1 tsp (5 mL)	1 tsp (5 mL)	1 tsp (5 mL)
1 tbsp (20 mL)	1 tbsp (15 mL)	1 tbsp (15 mL)

LINEAR MEASURES

5 mm	¼ in
1 cm	½ in
2 cm	¾ in
2.5 cm	1 in
5 cm	2 in
6 cm	2½ in
8 cm	3 in
10 cm	4 in
12 cm	5 in
15 cm	6 in
18 cm	7 in
20 cm	8 in
23 cm	9 in
25 cm	10 in
28 cm	11 in
30 cm	12 in
46 cm	18 in
50 cm	20 in
61 cm	24 in
77 cm	30 in

OVEN TEMPERATURES

	°C	°F	Gas Mark
Very slow	120	250	½
Slow	150	300	1–2
Mod. slow	160	325	3
Moderate	180	350	4
Mod. hot	190	375	5–6
Hot	200	400	6–7
Very hot	230	450	8–9

Glossary

Although the enjoyment of food is common to all nations, the names by which we know even the most common ingredients can vary from country to country. What Australians call a capsicum is a pepper in England and a bell pepper or sweet pepper in America. To compound the problem, food terms travel – with immigrants, foreign visitors and on food packaging – so even within one country, an item may be known by several different names. Consult the chart to locate an unfamiliar ingredient. Where there is no exact equivalent, an alternative may be suggested.

Australia	UK	US
Dairy Produce		
cream[1]	single cream	light cream
thickened cream	double cream	heavy cream
sour cream	soured cream	dairy sour cream
lard (animal origin)	lard (animal origin)	use shortening (vegetable origin)

[1]The range of creams sold commercially is constantly increasing. Crème fraîche is a cultured thick cream with a slightly sour tang.

Ingredients for Baking/Baked Goods and Pastry		
plain flour	plain flour	all-purpose flour[1]
self-raising flour	self-raising flour	self-rising flour
wholemeal flour	wholemeal flour	Graham/wholewheat flour
cornflour	cornflour	cornstarch
polenta/maize flour	yellow cornmeal	yellow cornmeal
bicarbonate of soda	bicarbonate of soda	baking soda
compressed yeast	fresh yeast	compressed yeast
white crystal sugar	white granulated sugar	white sugar[2]
caster sugar	caster sugar	superfine/extrafine sugar[2]
icing sugar	icing sugar	confectioners'/powdered sugar
demerara sugar	demerara sugar	use light brown sugar
raw sugar	use Muscovado sugar	use Turbinado sugar
golden syrup	golden syrup	use light corn syrup or maple syrup
molasses	use black treacle	molasses
cookie/biscuit	biscuit	cookie
golden oatmeal biscuits	use digestive biscuits	use Graham crackers
scone	scone	biscuit
sponge finger biscuit	boudoir biscuit	ladyfinger
shortcrust pastry	shortcrust pastry	basic pie dough
filo pastry	filo pastry	phyllo leaves

[1]American flour is finely milled - for baking, it may be necessary to add slightly more fat and liquid for similar results. [2]American regular sugar is finer than the UK equivalent; in most instances it can safely be substituted for caster sugar.

Nuts, Seeds and Grains		
copha	solid coconut cream	coconut butter
desiccated coconut	desiccated coconut	use shredded coconut
hazelnuts	hazelnuts	filberts/hazelnuts
pine nuts	pine nuts/pine kernels	pignoli/pinenuts
pepitas	dried untoasted pumpkin seeds	dried untoasted pumpkin seeds
burghul	bulgur/parboiled hulled cracked wheat	bulgur
cracked/kibbled wheat	cracked wheat	cracked wheat

Australia	UK	US
Fresh and Dried Fruit, Vegetables, Herbs and Aromatics		
currants	blackcurrants	black currants
custard apple	custard apple	cherimoya[1]
feijoa	feijoa	feijoa/pineapple guava
galangal	[2]	[2]
kiwifruit	kiwifruit	kiwi/Chinese gooseberry
papaya	pawpaw	papaya
passionfruit	passionfruit	passionfruit/purple granadilla
persimmon	use Sharon fruit	persimmon
rambutans[3]	use lychees	use litchis
rock melon	cantaloupe	cantaloupe
tamarillo[4]	tamarillo/tree tomato	tamarillo/tree tomato
glacé cherry	glacé cherry	candied cherry
sultana	sultana	golden/white raisin

[1]The term custard apple is used to describe a family of fruit including cherimoya, soursop and sweet sop. [2]Galangal is a rhizome resembling ginger but with a distinctly different flavour. It is not widely known in the UK or the US; ginger can be substituted, but the flavour will not be authentic. [3]Rambutans resemble lychees/litchis in flavour and are sometimes called hairy lychees, because the skin of the small oval fruit is covered with dark red-brown hairy spikes. [4]Tamarillos are smooth-skinned oval fruit, red or yellow in colour. The tough skin must be peeled before use.

Storecupboard Items		
cooking chocolate	cooking chocolate/Menière	unsweetened baking chocolate
dark chocolate	plain chocolate	semisweet chocolate
milk chocolate	milk chocolate	sweet chocolate
choc bits	use chocolate chips	use chocolate chips
chocolate vermicelli/hail	chocolate vermicelli	chocolate sprinkles
hundreds and thousands	hundreds and thousands	nonpareil
jelly crystals	jelly cubes	flavoured gelatin[1]
vanilla bean	vanilla pod	vanilla bean
vanilla essence	vanilla essence	vanilla extract[3]

[1]Jelly (the dessert, not the preserve) comes as crystals or cubes. Check package instructions when making up in case the amount of liquid required is different from that specified in recipes. [2]Vanilla essence/extract comes in different strengths; add to taste. Use natural vanilla essence where possible.

Appliances, Cookware and Paper Products		
absorbent paper	kitchen paper	paper towels
bar pan	loaf tin	loaf pan
double saucepan	double saucepan	double boiler
frying pan	frying pan	skillet
greaseproof paper	greaseproof paper	use waxed paper or baking parchment
griller	grill	broiler[1]
Lamington tin	28 x 18 cm /11 x 7 in baking tray, 4 cm/1½ in deep	28 x 18 cm/11 x 7 in baking tray, 4 cm/1½ in deep
patty cases	paper cake cases	cupcake papers
plastic wrap	cling film	plastic wrap
sandwich cake tin	sandwich cake tin	layer cake pan
springform tin	spring-release tin	springform pan
Swiss roll tin	Swiss roll tin	jelly roll pan
tea-towel	tea-towel	dish-towel
toothpick	cocktail stick	toothpick

[1]Australian and British cooks talk about grilling, Americans call it broiling; barbecued food is grilled in all three countries.

This edition published in 1995 by Leopard Books,
a division of Random House UK Ltd,
20 Vauxhall Bridge Road, London SW1V 2SA

First published in 1990 by Murdoch Books,
a division of Murdoch Magazines Pty Ltd,
213 Miller Street, North Sydney NSW 2060

Printed by New Interlitho, Italy
Typeset by Savage Type Pty Ltd, Brisbane, Qld

ISBN 0 7529 0156 7

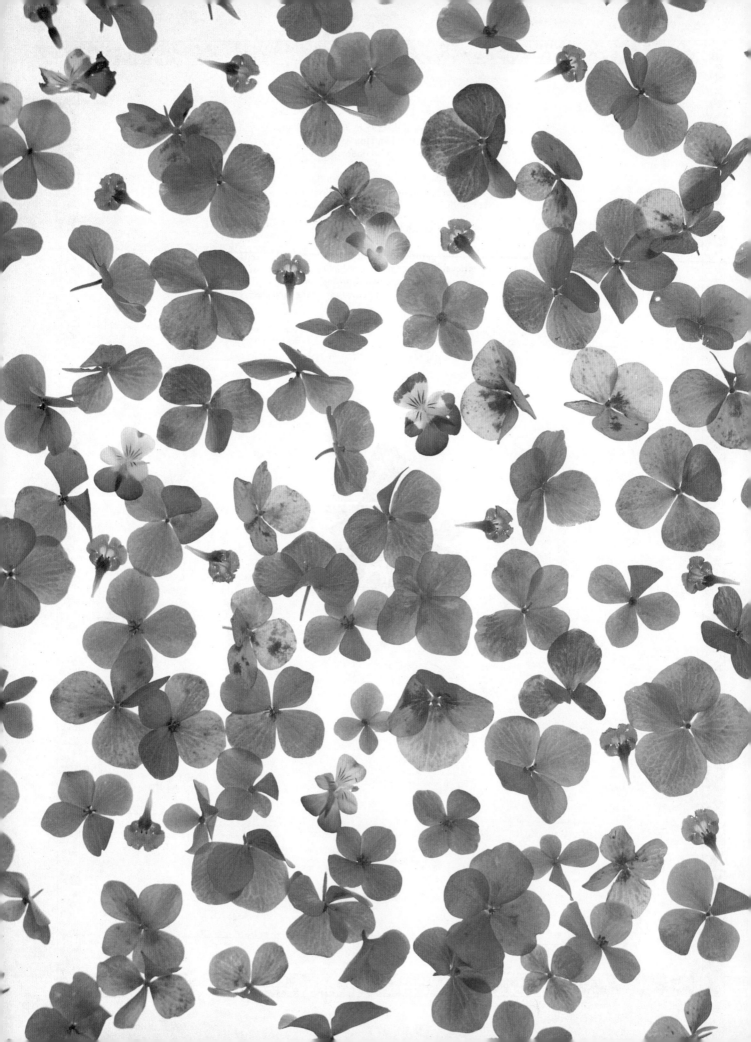